SEARCHING FOR SOLID GROUND

A Memoir

Reggie Harris
with Linda Hansell

Skinner House
Boston

www.skinnerhouse.org

Printed in the United States

Cover design by Eric Wilder
Cover image by Lana Brow/Shutterstock
Text design by Tim Holtz
Reggie Harris photo by Jeff Fasano Photography
Linda Hansell photo by Helen Aronson

print ISBN: 978-1-55896-925-4
eBook ISBN: 978-1-55896-926-1
Audiobook ISBN: 978-1-55896-927-8

6 5 4 3 2 1
27 26 25 24

Library of Congress Cataloging-in-Publication Data

Names: Harris, Reggie, 1952- author. | Hansell, Linda, author.
Title: Searching for solid ground : a memoir / Reggie Harris, with Linda Hansell.
Description: Boston : Skinner House, 2024. | Includes bibliographical references. | Summary: "In this captivating memoir, renowned musician Reggie Harris shares his journey from growing up as a low-income African American kid in Philadelphia to traveling the country and the world as a sought-after performer, educator, cultural ambassador and civil rights advocate. Searching for Solid Ground is filled with deeply personal stories and reflections of the author's life"-- Provided by publisher.
Identifiers: LCCN 2023056587 (print) | LCCN 2023056588 (ebook) | ISBN 9781558969254 (paperback) | ISBN 9781558969261 (ebook)
Subjects: LCSH: Harris, Reggie, 1952- | African American singers--Biography. | Singers--United States--Biography. | Civil rights workers--United States--Biography.
Classification: LCC ML420.H164 A3 2024 (print) | LCC ML420.H164 (ebook) | DDC 782.421642092 [B]--dc23/eng/20231207
LC record available at https://lccn.loc.gov/2023056587
LC ebook record available at https://lccn.loc.gov/2023056588

"Forgiving Our Fathers" by Dick Lourie reprinted from his collection *Ghost Radio* and accompanying CD *Ghost Radio Blues* (Hanging Loose Press, Brooklyn, New York, hangingloosepress.com).

Music changes the air.

—Bernice Johnson Reagon

CONTENTS

A NOTE ON LANGUAGE

Please note that this book follows the guidelines established by the Center for the Study of Social Policy in capitalizing the words Black and White when referring to race, as described in the article "Recognizing Race in Language: Why We Capitalize 'Black' and 'White.'"[1]

In the case of capitalizing *Black*, I agree with writer and professor Lori L. Tharps who states, "Black with a capital B refers to people of the African diaspora. Lowercase black is simply a color." Capitalizing Black also feels more respectful and more inclusive of the history of our people.

Capitalizing *White* is more complicated because it raises the specter of White supremacist movements. But ultimately it seems logical and equitable to capitalize both Black and White. Further, capitalizing White is a way of counteracting the disparity that the Center for the Study of Social Policy points out, "White people get to be 'just people,' without having their race named, whereas people of color are often described with their race."

In addition, I have deliberately and specifically used or quoted the terms African American, Black, colored people, and BIPOC (Black, Indigenous, and people of color) at different points throughout the book. My interchangeable usage is an outcome of what has been for me a long and often stressful

---

1   Recognizing Race in Language: Why We Capitalize 'Black' and 'White', Center for the Study of Social Policy, https://cssp.org/2020/03/recognizing-race-in -language-why-we-capitalize-black-and-white

journey that reflects the many-faceted nature of my people's struggle for freedom and self-determination. This evolution of terms was not only in the service of who we thought ourselves to be, but also reflective of the struggle with others who felt privileged and entitled to name us.

Language use, in racial circles, has always had the ability to create connections and restrictions, opinions and tensions. There are elements of both control and relationship. I was born into a world in which I was considered a "colored" or "Negro" child. These were the most respectful terms of reference that were available for our people to use. There were, of course, other terms, some still in use, that were used in alternative and/or negative ways. We were not always in control of those terms or able to dictate their use.

In my younger years, if anyone had referred to me or my friends as Black it would generally have been considered a reason for a fight. In those days that word, with colorism always a huge issue in the community, was considered an insult worthy of conflict or violence.

But in the 1960s and '70s, our younger, more confrontational leaders (with the help of James Brown's anthemic song) led a shift in self-determinational and nationalistic consciousness. They launched a movement of self-love and prideful appreciation that now had us saying "I'm Black and I'm Proud!" With that declaration, we slowly began to embrace the notion that "Black Is Beautiful." I will admit to being a slow convert to that movement. Calling myself Black did not come easily out of my mouth, or settle calmly in my mind. Over time, it became a more comfortable way for me to feel connected not only to our struggle here in the US but also to other BIPOC around the world. As my consciousness about "having a people" became a more visceral part of my awareness, Black became more than a color: it was a state of mind.

We continue to parse our understanding of who we are with shifts in language that now include Black American, BIPOC, and other evolving terms. I am represented in all of those terms in some ways, and by none of them completely. Each term used in this book has significance to me in different ways and reflects what I am trying to convey in each particular instance.

—Reggie Harris

PREFACE

Every now and then I step out of the day-to-day busyness (and business) of my life—rushing from one gig to another, writing and researching songs, scheduling new performances, leading civil rights tours through the South with the Living Legacy Project—and reflect on the fact that for the last forty-eight years, I have managed to make my living as a full-time touring musician, educator, and cultural ambassador. And I realize how extraordinary it is that I, an African American man from "da hood" in North Philadelphia, have been able to live this life of travel and performing, gaining access to a platform that makes an impact in the lives and perspectives of people all over the world. It has been an incredible journey. And it has not been an easy journey.

Performing as half of the duo Kim and Reggie Harris for forty-two years and then as a solo performer for the last six, there have been many triumphs and joyful moments—and many challenges and heartbreaks as well. The realities of racism and the uncertainty of "Touring While Black" made it necessary to face the cruelty and the stress of prejudice and racial hatred head-on. I've been put at risk and been disheartened by the relentless, insidious weight of oppression. I've had to gain skills to cope, navigate, negotiate, and educate, all in the effort to survive. The wounds are real and the cuts are deep, and the effort of surviving and trying to thrive as a Black man in America remains one of the most painful and enduring challenges of my life.

But through it all, I've also learned something about the power of resilience, the strength of community, and the soulful, inexhaustible brilliance of my people. As I reflect on my career, I'm aware that I have been driven by an invisible force that comes through my ancestors and allows me to use my musical gifts to be a bridge builder, a connector, and a promoter of justice. My family and my community raised me to understand that I had within me the creativity, grit, fortitude, and wisdom to withstand the fierce winds of derision and doubt and counseled me on ways to keep my essence and will intact. Their faith in me, and my cultural grounding, lit the flame that burns brightly in every fiber of my body, a flame that echoes those of Harriet, Frederick, Rosa, Martin, Ella, Malcolm, and so many less well-known sisters and brothers who paved the way before me.

Rev. Dr. Martin Luther King Jr. once said that he was a drum major for justice. In that same spirit, I have come to embrace the fact that I am a cultural ambassador for music, healing, and hope. Through sharing my music and my stories, and sometimes simply by being present in the room, I've been able to plant seeds of hope in the world. From a young age, I have sought to build bridges among people of different races. From the schools I attended, to the sports teams on which I played, to the places I have chosen to live, to the work that I have chosen to do, I have tried to build unity and impart hope.

Songs and stories are my method of spreading hope. They inform us, reconnect us to who we are, and connect us to each other. They impart lessons that make our lives more meaningful. And with context and reflection, they can show us what we might become: a society in which people of all races are treated with justice and dignity.

I love being a musician. I love the joy and power of singing and performing to create understanding among people. And I enjoy using music, when necessary, to disrupt the comfortable stasis that can cause us to settle into patterns of defensiveness and complacency. I try to do this respectfully, in an effort to encourage all of us—myself included—to consider and reconsider our points of view and hopefully to heal ourselves and our nation.

Music is the vehicle that re-energizes and reconnects me to the struggle and the joy. Music gives voice to the will and the wisdom of those ancestors on whose shoulders I stand. I sing so that others can find peace in their hearts and know that they are not alone. I sing because it is the balm that heals and makes us whole.

When Linda Hansell, my coauthor, approached me at a concert in February 2020, she said, "Have you ever thought about writing a memoir? You've led such an interesting life and have such remarkable stories to tell. I think you have a book inside of you." I chuckled and said, "You're not the first person to tell me that. But I don't know how to access it, or how to make that a reality." But lo and behold, with the time to write provided by a worldwide pandemic, an excellent writing partner to provide focus and organization, and a willingness to open myself and share what my heart has to offer, here is that book.

CHAPTER ONE

LET THERE BE MUSIC

My love of music began early. I sang at home starting when I was four or five years old with my mom and my sister Marlene. On Friday nights in our home in Philadelphia, we would gather at the piano to sing hymns and other songs until bedtime. With the TV turned off and Nana napping in her big chair, periodically waking to smile, we would take turns and share the verses on songs like "How Great Thou Art" or "Shall We Gather at the River." Occasionally, we'd sing a song by Harry Belafonte or a show tune from *South Pacific*, one of the few shows I remember my very religious mom taking us to see in the theater.

It was there that I began to learn how to trade harmonies, as my sister and I began to construct our own arrangements, with lyrics and antics that often earned us a raised eyebrow or a word of rebuke. It was a very happy time for me, and formative to my later years of singing in church and school choirs.

I did a lot of singing in church, the Nazarene Baptist Church at Nice and Lycoming Streets. My mother made sure we were in church as much as possible, usually arriving at least half an hour before the service started every Sunday. My church was a typical northern Black Baptist congregation, with a mix of working- and middle-class folks who loved a variety of music. We were "up and comin' colored folks" who sang spirituals in the old-school a cappella style as well as more classical, arranged spirituals by composers like Hall Johnson or Harry Burleigh. We also sang gospel songs, hymns, and anthems as a life-affirming way to connect with our ancestors. We demonstrated our strength just as our people had done since landing here in slave ships, bound and determined to show we had spiritual and moral depth.

The morning service started at 10:30 a.m. and would go on for about three hours. At 10:20, the organist would begin playing a prelude. Right on cue, one of our associate ministers would intone a call to worship, the organ would flair into the processional, and the choirs for that day, from an assortment of age-defined groups, would enter the sanctuary. As the choirs processed down the aisles, the congregation rose to its feet, singing in glorious harmony as the church filled with sound, floor to balcony. It took my breath away every single week.

I can still remember, actually still *feel*, the vibrant cacophony of sound that filled the air in that church. Voices primed and ready, calling out with passion. Hands and feet clapping in rhythm, drumming the wooden church floor in a joyful and sorrowful emotional release. It was a hopeful acknowledgment that we were all in it together. This is what my people have used to get through very hard times, and it grounded me in a sense of community that is both spiritual and cultural. It's what is often referred to as "having chuuch" in the vernacular. (The "r" is excluded for effect.)

At church, I felt embraced by and connected to my Black community in a weekly communion with the elders. The majestic spirit that filled that church is a recurring gift that continues to resonate in my body and inform my musical choices to this day.

It was in the children's choir that my public singing life started. I was one of the young church cherubs whose parents put them in the choir. Then, one Sunday at about age four, I was assigned to sing a solo on a song called "Sing Hosanna!"[2] I remember standing in my row, facing the rest of the church with my nervous little body shaking all over. I was fearful that I would forget some of the words, but I don't remember having fears about not hitting the notes. Although I was nervous, my voice was steadier than my torso. As rehearsed, I sang it out:

> Give me oil in my lamp, keep me burning
> Give me oil in my lamp I pray
> Give me oil in my lamp, keep me burning
> Keep me burning till the break of day

I finished the last phrase and heard shouts of "Amen!" and "Praise the Lord!" from the gathered throng. As I tried to settle myself back into the chorus to finish the rest of the song, I felt a rush of relief. Later, after the service, there were lots of pats on the back and head and compliments on my way to Sunday school that day.

I sang in the two church choirs reserved for youth, and starting in ninth grade I began taking voice lessons from Mrs. Gatling, the longtime church organist. She was a strict but

---

2 A. Sevison and C. Barny Robertson, "Oil in My Lamp." Lyrics copyright Capitol Christian Music Group, Capitol CMG Publishing, Universal Music Publishing Group.

loving force of nature who, as my voice and interests developed, allowed me to bring songs that I wanted to sing to my lessons, outside of the classical repertoire she preferred. I remember bringing her the song "Beautiful" and having to describe in detail who Gordon Lightfoot was, as he was not on her radar.

My musical roots also range back to second grade at Grover Cleveland Elementary School in North Philadelphia, where Miss Charlotte Churn, my teacher, used Woody Guthrie's song "This Land Is Your Land" to open a world of folk music and a wider world of discovery. It spoke of redwood trees, poverty and dust storms, and storied rivers, states, and people who were thousands of miles from my inner-city home in Philadelphia. That song shifted my point of view in ways that would not take true shape until I would have the chance, later in life, to travel and see them for myself. Miss Churn did her job as a teacher, expanding my mind by using a musical and cultural touchstone. She, like thousands of other dedicated educators, was trying to help her students find the space beyond the realms that our eyes could see and our locally focused brains could imagine.

(I was actually able to thank her for her efforts, quite unexpectedly, some thirty years later, when she unknowingly brought a class to one of my performances at the African American Museum in Philadelphia. When I approached her after the show, a graying, thirty-eight-year-old man standing before her, she chuckled and said, "I really must retire!")

Although I had expressed interest in playing a musical instrument in elementary school, the music teacher told me there weren't enough instruments to go around. When I asked again in middle school and requested to play the trumpet, I was told I could play the string bass. I gladly accepted that and played the bass for two years in seventh and eighth grades.

In eighth grade, a fortuitous event happened. At the time, I was attending a junior high school several neighborhoods away from my own. My homeroom and history teacher, Mr. Nicholas, asked my mother if he could make a recommendation for me to go to a high school that was also not in my neighborhood because, as he said, "Reginald is a very eclectic boy." (My mother would later misinterpret his use of that word by remarking, "He says that you talk too much!") He continued, "I think Reginald would do much better at the school that most of his fellow students will attend after finishing here, Olney High School."

My mom warily asked the coded question, "So it's a better school?" meaning, "So White kids go there?" And he said, "Yes!" That conversation and his subsequent intervention would be my ticket to options and accomplishments that my neighborhood school would likely not have afforded.

Looking back, I can now see that Mr. Nicholas, an African American male teacher in a school with a mostly White faculty, was following the same principle as the elders of my church and home community: Identify future leaders and connect them to better opportunities for advancement.

It was in high school that I encountered a number of teachers who guided me and helped me become who I am today: Ms. Hausler (homeroom in ninth grade), Mrs. Baker (English in tenth grade), Mr. Gerson (who saved me from the indignity of failing twelfth-grade physics with extra Saturday morning tutorial sessions), and the person who might be the single most important teacher in my finding a career in music, my choral director, Mr. Theodore Nitsche.

In my third week of ninth grade at Olney High School, I experienced one of those moments that, looking back, I recognize as a pivotal event. I was sitting with hundreds of other students in the auditorium, awaiting an address from the principal, when the Olney High School a cappella choir walked in, gathered in two groups at the front and rear of the auditorium, and sang one song. Just one! But that song, "Echo Song" by Orlando di Lasso, spoke to me so strongly that my only thought was, "I need to be in that choir!"

Later that day, I went up to the fifth floor to see Mr. Nitsche, the music teacher, who had started teaching at Olney the day the school opened in 1936. The choir was his pride and joy. I began my mission by informing him that he needed me in his choir. The news was not good: he told me that I had missed the choir auditions by one week and that the choir roster was set. In an unusually bold move for me, I informed him that he needed me because I was a tenor and he didn't have enough. (I had counted nine tenors in a 100-voice choir.) He stared at me, and said "Really?" After a brief conversation, he took me in a rehearsal room and gave me a quick vocal test. In minutes, I became tenor number ten. That moment and my subsequent four years as part of the choir family changed my life in many ways, both in my time as a student at that school and even more in my journey as a person, an educator, and a musician.

Mr. Nitsche was an unusual man. He was serious about music, about personal and community responsibility, and about getting the music right through being expressive and precise. He thought of all of us as "his kids" and, when we misbehaved, "his rousters" (a term already out of use even by that time). He was a Quaker and a firm believer in the worth of all individuals, though he could be opinionated and sharp when talking about "evildoers" and bad behavior. His talks usually centered on compassion and responsibility, as he constantly lectured us about the need to be good role models in the world. For a kid who was dealing with many issues both at home and at school, facing situations where race, religion, and class issues made me feel inferior, he proved on any number of occasions that he saw and appreciated me for who I was. (And that even carried over to the times when I got on his last nerve!) In his choir I made friends who would eventually connect me to people and places that helped me discover my voice in new ways, learn the guitar, and become the musician I am today.

Most of my joyful memories about high school revolve around my time in the choir. One of the hallmarks of my time at Olney was being part of the traveling choir. Every year, Mr. Nitsche would choose twenty-four choir members to form a small group that he could use to sing at events around the neighborhood and at special events around the city. We would rehearse on Friday afternoons from 2:30 until 4:00 or 4:30.

Between the a cappella choir, the traveling choir, and my voice lessons with Mrs. Gatling, I now got a solid dose of classical repertoire such as Bach, Handel, and Mozart, spirituals by Black composers like Hall Johnson or Moses Hogan (also sung at my church), contemporary music by composers like Randall Thompson, songs from musicals, and folk songs. This cornucopia of sound and musical textures was glorious. I couldn't get enough of the harmonic rapture, the dissonant collisions, and the myriad ways that parts and harmonies could be formed, arranged, and resolved in any piece of music. Within a short time, I made it my business to learn all the parts and then sing them either with the sections in rehearsal or in my head throughout the day. It was an unofficial master class in arranging and composition.

Choir rehearsals, and in particular Friday afternoon sessions with the traveling choir, were both marvelously hard work and a time of special camaraderie. Mr. Nitsche turned out to be a master at creating a community of singers whose voices blended and formed a cohesive wave of sound. Those traveling choir events also introduced me to new sections of Philadelphia and to a wider range of places, religions, and people than I would ever have encountered. I was becoming a citizen of the wider world.

This widened world was not without its degree of stress and trauma. I was a poor Black kid going to school outside of my neighborhood, moving into an environment where even the other Black kids, students from the Mount Airy and Oak Lane sections of Philly, would turn their noses up at a kid from Tioga-Nicetown, only streets away from the "ghetto." To keep other students from judging me, I told no one where I lived for the entire four years. I felt ashamed of my social location, my lack of financial resources, and my limited wardrobe.

But my cover was blown one night when Mr. Nitsche drove me and a few other choir kids home after one Sunday night concert. Earlier that fall, my mom had accompanied me to a concert at one of the big Lutheran churches near the school. After our performance, my mother told Mr. Nitsche how much she loved the concert and that she appreciated his confidence in me. She wanted me to participate in as many concerts with the choir as possible, but impressed on him that we lived far away, and that given the limited nature of weekend public transportation she was worried about my traveling to such events by myself, particularly coming home after dark. As I stood trying to get her to leave, lest she give away too much information, he praised me and said, "I want Reginald to be with us as often as possible, and I promise you that if he can get himself to a concert, I will make certain to get him home to your door."

A few weeks later, after another evening engagement, Mr. Nitsche sought me out and said, "I promised your mother that I would take you home, so you stay close by me until we are all ready to leave."

"*All* ready to leave?" My brain kicked into gear. Who was "all?"

By the time things got sorted out, Mr. Nitsche's Volkswagen bug was filled with five other students whose parents he had also promised to drop at their door. My problem was that most of them lived fairly close to him. He decided that since I lived the farthest away, he would give everyone a treat and make this a fun road trip. I was mortified.

As soon as we were in the car, I started to work on him to get him to drop me at the subway. "Oh no, you rouster! I promised your mother that I'd bring you to her door, and that's what I'm going to do!" Two more tries at a diversionary drop went unheeded, and soon he was giving us all a historic tour as we crossed neighborhoods and passed stores and churches, getting closer to the area I didn't want these kids to see.

As we got closer to my neighborhood, the other kids in the car got more interested in where we were going, and I could see that some of them were getting a little nervous.

"Where are we going, Mr. Nitsche?" one of them asked.

"Reginald lives in Nicetown!" he replied, and recited some historic facts about the area.

As we crossed Broad Street, he continued to entertain as the other kids got quieter and quieter. We passed the railyards at Wayne Junction and sped across Hunting Park Avenue, finally arriving on my block.

My street was filled with homes of proud working-class Black families. The homes were mostly well maintained, but they were big, older houses, kept up by hard-working people. There was only one tree on our block, compared to the more tree-lined streets where most of those kids lived. I had seen where some of them lived, and my North Philly rowhouse was a far cry from their homes. This was foreign territory for them.

Upon arriving at my house, Mr. Nitsche said to the car filled with fearful, gawking White choir kids, "Young people, that is the beautiful home where our marvelous Reginald lives." And that was one of the most amazing gifts that any teacher would give me in all of my years of schooling.

The next day, none of those kids mentioned our trip to Nicetown, and they were all still my friends. It would take years for me to deal with being "from poverty" and to learn that having dated clothes or not living in the "right place" didn't have to define me. But that night started the healing of my heart in a big way. Theodore Nitsche was a remarkable man.

During our rehearsals Mr. Nitsche would sometimes go on at length, talking to us with sincere intensity about matters of right and wrong. Seeing our puzzled faces staring blankly back at him, he would smile and say, "Oh, what am I to do with you?" He would then pronounce, "Turn and face the windows!"

Having practiced this move week after week, we would turn and face the gorgeous sunset shining through the tall bank of cathedral windows at the back of the choir loft that overlooked the surrounding neighborhood as he, or one of our accompanists, would intone a chord. Then, in studied cadence, we would sing a glorious four-part arrangement of English composer John Milford Rutter's "The Lord Bless You and Keep You," with its seven-part Amen, into the fading light of the day. This was a song he'd used as a signature piece with every Olney High choir he led.

Mr. Nitsche passed away in 1979. Upon hearing of his death, I found myself in attendance one evening at a Quaker meeting in the Philadelphia suburb of Abington, Pennsylvania, for his memorial service, along with a number of past Olney High School choir members. After silence, eulogy, and wonderful and amusing remembrances had been offered, I heard someone say to the gathered group, "Turn and face the windows!" And just as we had all been trained to do during so many rehearsals, and as we had done in performance after performance, we began to sing that marvelous arrangement one more time to honor our dear departed mentor. It remains one of my most treasured memories.

Mr. Nitsche and the other teachers I mentioned made me feel capable, safe, challenged, and more confident. They lit a fire in me for striving, observing carefully, listening with purpose, and sharing my opinions. Singing in the high school choir ignited in me a love of singing Bach choral works and learning to use counterpoint in ways that still inform my choices every time I harmonize. I can't help but be grateful for the inspiration those teachers helped me claim as my own. Looking back, I see clearly how they sparked a passion for questioning, learning, and exploring that led me to use my curiosity and gifts to become the person I am.

CHAPTER TWO

ACROSS THE GREAT DIVIDE

I realized early in life that having brown skin would be an everyday challenge in America. Ever since, racial issues have been a natural part of my landscape; they are the mountains, canyons, and plains of my daily existence. And as a Black man in America, they have often been matters of life and death. I have been the target of acts of racial insensitivity, verbal abuse, police harassment, internalized oppression, inter-community violence, race-based terror, and other forms of prejudice my entire life. My body and my psyche bear the scars of the stress and disease (and dis-ease) caused by pervasive and persistent discrimination, racism, and profiling.

I grew up in a neighborhood where there was a relative degree of safety due to the fact that it was predominantly Black, or "colored" (as African Americans were called in those days), by the time I came to live there in the mid-1950s. Many years earlier, my grandfather and grandmother, who migrated from Virginia in the early years of the Great Black Migration, managed to buy a house in the Nicetown-Tioga section of Philadelphia, which was at that time an all-White neighborhood.

My grandfather had found work as a driver and a mechanic for some well-to-do White Philadelphia families. (Rumor has it that he worked for the Strawbridge family of the Philadelphia department store Strawbridge & Clothier fame.) This work gave him the access and money to start his own auto garage. It also helped him learn about different areas of the city. That is most likely how he came to notice the home on 17th Street that he decided he wanted to buy.

One of my early memories of living in that house was a woman visitor who would drop by our house periodically, always unannounced. Well-dressed and friendly but a little formal, her appearance always sparked a joyful reaction from my mom and grandmom. Her actual relationship was never explained to me and my sister, and I assumed she was a relative. She never failed to take a great interest in questioning us.

"Look at these fine children, growing so big. Are you two young people studying hard in school?" she would ask with a smile.

"Yes ma'am!" we would dutifully respond.

"Well, that's good. That's the only way you'll grow up to be something in the world!" she would reply. After a few more minutes of conversation, she would be on her way and life would resume as usual.

I would learn much later from my mother that her name was Juanita Kidd Stout, a successful lawyer in the district attorney's office in Philadelphia who went on to become both a municipal court judge and a judge on the Pennsylvania Supreme Court, the first African American woman to serve in both those roles, and the first African American woman to be appointed to a Supreme Court in any state. Judge Stout, I learned, had arranged for the secret purchase of the house with the help of a White realtor years before my birth. In those days (and sometimes even now) a Black family couldn't just buy a home anywhere they wanted. Somehow, my grandfather made a connection with this prominent Black female lawyer, and she helped them buy the house.

When my grandparents first moved in, they were the first Black family on the block. After they arrived, as often happened across the nation, White flight shifted the demographic status of many sections of the city, as White families fled to escape the perceived downgrading of their neighborhoods. By the time I moved into that house at age one or two when my parents divorced, the racial composition of the neighborhood had completely changed, and therefore I began life sheltered inside that working-class Black community with church, school, and my Black playmates as a background to the wider world of northern segregation. We encountered White people, but generally it would be in controlled circumstances on trips to the market or on public transportation. There were two exceptions to the White flight—an Italian family that decided to stay in their home in the middle of the block, and a Jewish family that owned the small grocery store on the corner where we did most of our mid-week incidental food shopping. One of the daughters in that family tutored me in Algebra in high school to my benefit and, as I remember, her frustration.

Despite being kept safe from many harms, there were constant reminders throughout my childhood that we were "other" in the frame of who mattered in America. Some of those messages came from TV, newspapers, and magazines that largely chose not to show constructive images and stories about Black people. In the mainstream media, it seemed that any positive, prominent, or noteworthy people were White. As a counter to that we had our own newspapers (the *Tribune* in Philly) and magazines (*Ebony* and *Jet*) that reported the impactful and cultural news of "colored folks." In school and in our history books we learned almost exclusively about White people, with the possible exception of Frederick Douglass or George Washington Carver (the peanut guy). Presidents, explorers, statesmen, doctors, scientists—all of them White. Black history as a subject of study or import was well in the future. Of course, there were many Black sports stars and entertainers, since White people felt comfortable with us in those roles, and a few notable political leaders such as Dr. Martin Luther King Jr., A. Phillip Randolph (the man who was responsible for the idea of the March on Washington in 1963), and the very controversial Malcolm X. While they were certainly in the news, they were not necessarily seen as people who were helping our nation to progress—each for different reasons.

From a tender age, I became used to the local police treating us Black boys as potential perpetrators of future crime. Instead of a "How ya doin', boys?" as a greeting from a passing cop, we were more likely to hear a snarled "What are you little hoodlums up to?" Although I was young, this negative characterization of boys like me began to seep into my consciousness and create an uncomfortable feeling in my body. "Why do they see us differently than the White boys?" I wondered. Seeing a police officer, most of whom were White, produced feelings of anxiety, and I avoided them whenever possible. The fear of an encounter with the law was present long before I began to drive as a teen.

Ironically, in my elementary school, our teachers taught us to sing songs that suggested "Go up to your kind policeman, the very first one you see" as advice to follow if we were lost or confused. But my friends and I learned early on that approaching a cop was about the last thing you wanted to do.

There were also encounters with some of the White salesmen who came into our neighborhood to sell appliances, insurance, and other products door to door. They were taking advantage of the fact that most people in our neighborhood suffered from a lack of access to buying those items at sales offices or on credit at major stores. If we were playing outside when the salesmen parked their cars, some would greet us with a smile and say "Hello!" while others would act nervously in our presence and warn us against "messing with their car" while they were attending to their business. Not exactly the way to earn our trust. The two White salesman that frequented my house were always very nice and talked to me and my family with respect.

There were lots of mixed messages coming my way in those early years, as the adults I knew used coded language to guide us kids through potential problem situations. They would warn us, if we were being too boisterous in public or seemingly out of control and "on display," that punishment would be severe. "I'll slap the Black off you!" they'd say, or inform us that "You're actin' like a Negro!" That term had many meanings, both positive and negative.

It wasn't unusual for a Black adult to tell a misbehaving child "You *know* you know better! You *know* that you got to represent!" It was their way of letting us know that it was our job, just like all other "colored" folks, to make sure White people had no reason to think we were not "civilized" or worthy of being allowed into stores or establishments where White people shopped. Unacceptable behavior was often met with harsh treatment—a rough grab or a whack on the butt—to show nearby White shoppers that they could relax and not be worried that these Black folks and their kids might make a scene. Our folks took care of discipline quickly and visibly so that White folks didn't have to step in to take care of the "problem." Friends and historical accounts tell me that it was often much worse in the South.

To hear our parents speak as if being Black was a bad thing that needed erasure or correcting was confusing, to say the least. What I know now is that they were giving us lessons and warnings about a world that would be inhospitable and unforgiving. It was also an introduction to the internalized oppression that plagues marginalized communities, conveying the notion that, deep down, my people and I are inferior.

Out of sight or hearing of White people, they would say things like, "You know how *they* are! Don't give them a reason." There was much that we were required to know about how to behave and live in a White-majority society. We listened and obeyed but largely didn't understand the depth of their message. It became clearer when the more deeply scarring experiences came after age thirteen or so.

The street I grew up on, 17th Street, is a major North-South artery in Philadelphia that runs the length of the city. There was always a lot of traffic—both cars and buses—running by my home all day long. This brought a diverse stream of travelers through our neighborhood every day. On summer nights, as soon as the major league baseball season began, race and class collisions came right past my door. Connie Mack stadium, where the Philadelphia Phillies played their home games at the time, was less than two miles down the street on

Lehigh Avenue. When the Phillies were home, tour bus after tour bus would go rumbling past my house for hours, bringing fans from places like Scranton, Wilkes-Barre, Lewistown, Bloomsburg, and other Pennsylvania towns into the city, on their way to enjoy a game.

The passengers on those buses, White Phillies fans of every age, suddenly found themselves traveling through North Philly, which I'm sure for them was a harrowing trip through what they knew as "the ghetto." Quite often, the line of buses would get backed up at the traffic light on Erie Avenue at the end of the block waiting for the next green light. That pause subjected the passengers on the buses and those of us playing on the street or sitting on porches to an involuntary intercultural moment in time. The looks on many of their faces revealed complete and utter dismay about being, even briefly, exposed to the perceived danger of difference. These brief episodes usually lasted no more than three minutes, and most passed without incident. But every now and again, particularly on buses where the air conditioning was not engaged, some comments or facial expressions, friendly and otherwise, might be exchanged. I have enduring memories of kids and/or adults on the bus waving to us with friendly smiles that created distant but heartfelt goodwill. Sadly, I also have about as many memories of angry, puzzled faces with frowns or tongues stuck out in derision. At the changing of the light, the buses would move on, leaving us all with an unsettled feeling that we stored away for another time. In many ways, those interactions frame the ongoing tension of life in America, with different communities living in separate worlds of perception.

I attended junior high and high school outside of my

neighborhood, and it was then that I began to experience more personally scarring racial incidents. Jay Cooke Junior High was a mostly White school in an all-White neighborhood called Logan. Philadelphia schools were being integrated, though I don't remember anyone ever saying that word out loud. Similarly, no one warned me that White kids and neighborhood residents would react to me with hostility simply because I had brown skin.

With a multiracial faculty that included one of the members of my church, Jay Cooke Junior High School was known as a "good school" in a "good neighborhood," and the principal and staff kept a pretty tight rein on us. I noticed that the neighborhood surrounding the school had nicer homes, wider streets, and more trees. It was a softer environment that felt less busy and cluttered than my own.

At that school, the prejudice from the White students was subtle and at times hard to figure out. Kids might play with you just fine one day and then, faced with opposition from their White friends or students from a different section, might not want to know you on another.

Often when playing schoolyard games during recess or after school, I would be challenged to fight. Fights in the schoolyard were common, even though teachers were obviously looking to prevent incidents. But I only ever got into two fights. One of them happened when a White boy started yelling at me during recess as his White friends egged him on. I kept talking to him, trying to ask what I had done to cause this, but he was clearly responding to outward pressure that left him unable to give any explanation for his actions. Before we actually struck blows, a teacher came over to break up the confrontation.

Other fights broke out weekly in the early part of the school year but lessened as the year went on. Through good modeling by the teachers and shared work environments, we began to discover that regardless of color, some kids were fun to be with and others were jerks.

It was at that school that I began to understand that I had some innate skills and a personality that, in difficult situations, could connect with people and help mitigate racial tensions. This made me feel powerful and good about myself, especially because I was reluctant to speak up in or out of class. I didn't see myself as a leader in class at that point. That would change with time.

Maybe because I was on the bottom rung of the leadership ladder in our seventh-grade class, I noticed the tension that existed between the various sections of the grade. I'm not certain how the school put sections together, but there were some ethnic, class, and other differences that became apparent to me from seeing who was in each section. For whatever reason (maybe GPA?) section 7-2 had fewer athletes and more "smart kids," many of whom happened to be White and/or Jewish. I never saw their grades, but they presented as kids who usually did well in school. And the opposite was true of kids in the higher-numbered sections, who I remember as being grouped in sections 7-12 and 7-14. These sections had more kids of color and more kids who were competitive or "boisterous." (I was in section 7-8, in the middle.) During football season, after I started to get some playing time, I began to develop friendships with—or at the very least talk to—kids in those other sections. I was able to break down some of the animosity that could arise during our cross-section interactions. The extended connections gave me more kids to play with during recess, as I would often be invited into boxball or other games that were started by kids from other sections. It wasn't something I planned out or was conscious of at the time. But my desire to reach out came naturally, so I followed it. Looking back, it was an early start to getting comfortable making entrance to groups to which I did not belong.

I don't remember being called an epithet or having a White classmate openly demean me by race in junior high, as happened many, many times in high school. People in the area would periodically call out hurtful words from their houses and porches as I walked by. Sometimes store owners in the area addressed us "colored" kids more roughly or waited on the White kids before us. In high school I did encounter hostile reactions or name calling, such as being called the N-word in subway cars or buses traveling to South Philadelphia, a largely Italian and Irish enclave, or the Northeast section of the city. I began to understand that I needed to be more aware as I moved about. But for the most part I was oblivious to the danger, as young people can be, and took most of what happened in stride.

I did learn to avoid the obvious bullies when necessary (which was true in elementary school too), and I was very adept at running away quickly whenever the need arose. In those days, before guns entered the equation, flight on foot was always an option to get away from a dangerous situation, like one I encountered one day in eighth grade on the way home from school. That day I saw a group of White boys sizing me up as I approached my trolley stop, half a block away. Always on alert, I didn't wait for them to make their move and was gone, books and all, tracking toward the next station while checking over my shoulder to make sure they were giving up the chase. Fortunately, the next stop was only five blocks south of where I started.

The problems didn't only come from White folks. At one point in my ninth-grade year, a Black kid named Sam who lived around the corner accosted me as I was running an errand for Nana to the Chicken Store, the White-owned poultry and egg shop that was a mainstay in the neighborhood. Sam came up behind me and yelled, "Hey, punk! I heard from Tony"—another kid from the neighborhood who went to my school—"that you up at that White school trying to become a White boy!"

"News to me!" I spat out.

Tony and I barely knew each other, though he was in my German language class. I'd been trying to get used to the fact that, as a Black kid at a school many neighborhoods away, I was out of my comfort zone much of the time. But I hadn't shared any of that with Tony or anyone from around my way.

Sam and I had been on good terms up until then, but nothing I said seemed to matter to him now. Without warning, he began to pummel me with punches, which I was fortunately able to block (due to my fascination with boxing at the time) until an older guy I knew came through an alley and intervened. Sam promised me that he would "be waiting for me after school every day 'til I can make you sorry you sold us out!" This threat prompted me to make certain that I never came home from school at the same time or from the same direction for that entire school year. Fortunately, Sam's family moved away that next summer.

In addition, Black gangs were beginning to be a problem in the neighborhood, and those groups of boys would roam around at night looking for stray kids to harass and beat up. If you were unlucky enough to run into one of these roving units, you would be asked the phase that froze you in your tracks: "Where you from?" Meaning, what gang do you belong to? And as you might imagine, there was no right answer, unless you somehow knew one of them personally. "Hey, that's my boy, Reggie," a friend or acquaintance might offer. "I know him from the playground up on the avenue. He's cool!" And you'd be free to go. On the occasions that I couldn't run away, the best defense was acting dumb or talking crazy and hoping they showed you some mercy and didn't have a need to beat you up that day.

One morning, Nana woke me from a sound sleep. As soon as I heard her voice, I realized I had overslept. I jumped out of bed, threw on my clothes, and rushed from the house, knowing that I would be off schedule for my public transportation. On my way out, I grabbed my small lunch bag containing my lunch, which fortunately I'd had the foresight to make the night before.

That small bag that contained my favorite lunch in the world—some potato chips, a piece of fruit, and a sandwich made of one scrambled egg, cheese, mustard, mayo, and two slices of Taylor pork roll. (For the uninitiated, Taylor pork roll is a processed meat treat similar to bologna—but much, *much* better—that is commonly available from delis in Philadelphia, New Jersey, and several neighboring states. It was developed in 1856 by John Taylor of Trenton and sold as Taylor's Prepared Ham until 1906. Many people in Pennsylvania and New Jersey still refer to it as "Taylor ham.")

Lunch bag in hand, I ran to the corner of 17th and Erie Avenue where, upon seeing no trolley car in sight, I ran the three long blocks to Broad Street and sprinted down the stairs into the dark recesses of the subway. On the way down the stairs, I heard a train pulling into in the station and, without thinking, ran down onto the platform, only to discover that the sound was from a southbound train. Looking up the tracks, I could see that I had just missed a northbound train by seconds and now would have to wait for the next train to go the three stops that would take me to Wyoming Avenue and Cooke Jr. High. For now, I stood alone on the platform.

I was not alone for long. Suddenly, from around the back of a staircase, I watched as five Black boys, slightly older than me, slowly appeared and walked to where I was standing. I knew that groups of boys often hung around subway stations waiting out of the sight of subway personnel and would demand small change from kids on their way to school, and maybe beat them up. Usually, if I knew there was no train, I would wait on the upper level until one pulled into the station. In my hurry, I had not followed that protocol.

"Where you from?" came the familiar question.

I froze. I wanted to run back upstairs where I would be in sight of the cashier's booth, but the boys strategically stood between me and the closest staircase.

"Nowhere!" I gave the answer that was one of the only hopeful choices for a non-gang-related kid.

"Give me your money," said the boy who seem to be the leader.

"I don't have any money," I replied truthfully.

After sizing me up, with the other boys glaring and

awaiting some signal for action, the leader boy said, "What's in the bag?"

"My lunch!"

"Give it to me."

I was trembling, but I knew in my heart that I was unwilling to lose that sandwich. Having no money meant that I would go hungry for the whole day. *And* it was a Taylor pork roll sandwich, something my mother knew I loved but could only afford to buy every now and then. It was time to make a stand.

"No!" I said with a slight raise in my voice. "This is a Taylor pork roll sandwich and it's my lunch and you can't have it."

All the other boys laughed out loud, but the leader boy stepped forward, pushed me, and grabbed the bag. As the other boys also stepped forward, he opened the bag and looked inside.

"It's a fucking sandwich!" He blurted out. He looked at me incredulously. "You're willing to get beat up for a fucking sandwich?"

I wasn't quite sure what to say. "It's my favorite sandwich. And it's my lunch!"

The boys looked at each other and then all laughed as the leader closed the bag. Looking me in the eye, he threw the bag down on the tracks.

"Crazy motherfucker!" he sneered as they all walked down the platform, up the steps, and disappeared.

I stood there watching them walk away with my heart racing, trying to calm down. I looked down on the tracks and saw that the sandwich bag had landed in a dry spot between the rails. Peering down the tracks, I saw no lights in the distance. There might be time—if I hurried.

I ran to the end of the platform and quickly scurried down the steps and onto the tracks. Terrified that the train might suddenly appear without warning, I raced to the spot and grabbed the bag. With no delay, I ran back to the stairs and, careful not to come in contact with the third rail, bounded up the steps and back onto the platform. Moments later, the train arrived.

Still slightly ruffled and unsteady, I got on the train, bag and books in hand, and I was on my way to school. I was lucky they hadn't decided to beat me up. I now find it hard to believe that I faced down a pack of boys over a pork roll sandwich, but on that day, my lunch was worth standing up for.

Dealing with the provocations and threats of violence that came from both White and Black people was a central challenge of my youth and made me feel caught in the middle. The muggings and threats from Black gang members made it difficult for me to fully embrace my own race, despite my strong ties to my church community. It made me question my place in the world and my racial identity. As a result, internalized oppression, like a demon on my shoulder, became an ever-present voice in my daily narrative.

CHAPTER THREE

PICKLE IN THE MIDDLE

In high school, racial tensions came into view in a much more vivid, intense, and powerful way. As my peers and I came of age, with hormones raging and our brains more attuned to the unrest gripping Philly and the nation in the late 1960s, relationships at school began to mimic the larger community. Not being from a politically active family, I was not always aware of the cultural shifts that were taking place.

For example, in tenth grade I was completely unaware of the nonviolent, student-led protests against injustice and the lack of Black history instruction that hit the Philadelphia Board of Education in 1967. Those student protests led to some brutal retaliation and beatings of the demonstrating high school students by the police, a response typical of then-Chief of Police Frank Rizzo's violent approach to policing. (The School Board eventually engaged with and agreed to the student demands.)

The fallout from that protest and police response came to my high school in the form of a three-day sit-in by Black students, without my knowledge or participation. I happened upon it by accident on the third day while passing through the marble hallway outside the auditorium in which the sit-in was happening. I ran into a Black girl from one of my classes at the door of the auditorium.

"Oh, you finally coming to join us?"

"Join you for what?" I asked, perplexed.

"Oh, that figures," she snorted, and closed the door in my face. I was curious about what was going on, but I continued on to class, and then to lunch.

As news of the police action downtown came to the students involved in the sit-in at my school, tempers flared and they left the auditorium and headed for the lunchroom. Once there, they came upon some White students, and words were exchanged and fists began to fly. During the escalation, I watched a Black student respond to a comment by a White student by hitting him over the head with a lunch tray. Within seconds, that melee erupted into a full-scale race riot that brought the full force of the Philadelphia police (who had been stationed outside the school) storming into our building. With no restraint, Rizzo's troops started beating and arresting students all over the building, as they had in confrontations with students elsewhere in the city.

I had been eating lunch with five or six of my White friends from the choir, sitting mere feet from the flashpoint. I could see that they were terrified by the violence and the discomforting presence of the riot-gear-wearing cops, but I was strangely calm. We were approached by a plainclothes officer who tersely instructed us to "Leave. Now!" I remember testing him by asking, "Can we finish our ice cream?" which brought a glaring smirk and a curt, "I don't think so. Get out and take your friends with you."

Seeing the fearful confusion of my friends, and feeling like I had some knowledge that could be useful to them, I volunteered to lead the group of White choir kids from the lunchroom to a safer spot. For some reason, I felt empowered to play an authoritative and protective role. My immediate thought was to get them to the choral room, an out-of-the-way location on the fifth floor where most students wouldn't think to go. We set out on our escape journey and reached the room safely using an alternate set of stairs. Our choir director Mr. Nitsche was in the room, and once we arrived he offered to lock the door, which quieted the other students.

On our way to the choir room, we had passed some students in the halls, both Black and White, who saw me and said, "Reggie, there are kids who are looking for you because you've got too many friends on both sides. You need to get out of the building. People want to hurt you."

I don't know how my name came up, but I took that as a credible warning. Once my choir friends were safe, I chose to get out of the school and go home, using a little-known exit in the basement through the boiler room. (It was the one we used on Friday afternoons when choir practice ended after the school's main doors were locked at 4:00 p.m.)

That frightening episode got me thinking. Up to that point, having both Black friends and White friends didn't seem like a big deal. I had been focused on getting to know people and making connections with people on the basis of who they were, not their color. I didn't realize that people cared or had even noticed who I was friends with, and I was totally ignorant of the issues that many of my Black peers were focused on. Now I found myself suddenly sandwiched between the two sides. Without being conscious of it, I was already acting as a bridge across the color line. I was also naïve about there being no consequences for that, and I needed to wake up.

The school was closed for three days after the riot. During that time at home, I began to ask myself some questions. *Why am I in danger for being in the middle? All I've tried to do during my time here at Olney is make friends and follow my mother's good advice to love everyone. What is all this injustice that is stoking the fire of rage in students my age? What am I missing that has separated me from those Black students who ended up in the protests and in jail? Am I really trying to be White?*

During my four years at Olney I made lots of friends, eventually being voted best personality (along with a girl named Karen) in my graduating class of 1970. I saw myself as a bridge-builder, but perhaps my Black peers saw me as not being loyal to the race. This would account for what my neighbor Sam had been telling me when he said I was "trying to sell us out." And why Black kids at Olney wanted to hurt me. Just being friends with both Black and White people, being willing to talk to them and see them as equals and individuals, had put me at risk once the lines were drawn. This added to my confusion and sense of isolation.

The race riot, and the fact that I had been a target, greatly heightened my awareness of racial tension between Black people and White people across the nation. I started reading the *Philadelphia Inquirer* and watching the evening news, and I became somewhat aware that there was an upheaval going on in the country. I didn't know about the more violent confrontations, even though a number of them were going on right in Philly, in some cases just twenty to thirty blocks away from my house. There were no clarifying conversations at home or at church related to the struggles that were raging. While I was operating with very little real knowledge of the historical or current struggles of Black folks North or South, I did at least know that those of us with brown skin seemed to make a lot of White people crazy, and that having dark skin made our lives harder.

There were many issues that were negatively impacting the Black community around us in Philadelphia. One of them was a lack of access to well-paying driver, salesman, and factory jobs, which led to a boycott of the Tasty Baking Company by African Americans. It was led by Reverend Leon H. Sullivan, a man I knew tangentially, whose prominent church on Broad Street was mere blocks from my house and was linked with my church. Reverend Sullivan headed a group called 400 Ministers that initiated activism on issues affecting the Black community throughout the city—housing segregation, educational inequity, the tiny percentage (less than one percent) of private sector jobs involving contact with customers in Philadelphia that were held by African Americans, and the exclusion of African Americans from Girard College, a private school in North Philadelphia.

These protests took place out of my personal purview, since my family and church were not active in the simmering political struggle. In many ways I was very sheltered, growing up in a house that was focused on religion and on just trying to make it through. We were not a family that attended protests or marches. The message at our Baptist Church on so many Sundays was Love. Love thy neighbor. The message from both church and home was the golden rule: Treat others as you wish to be treated. Respect everyone.

At home and at church, the folks just kept praying and following "God's will," convinced that our faith in "letting go and letting God" would solve these decades-old racial inequities. I remember that we got warnings from our pastor and from church leaders that those folks who were protesting were not doing God's will—by which he meant working nonstop to get people "saved."

Rather than engaging in protests, my mother and grandmother focused on teaching me and my sister to work hard and treat people well. That was one of their missions in life, and I feel that their focus has given me a helpful vantage point for looking at racial issues. Despite her financial and class status, Mom always carried herself with an air of pride and dignity. She did not allow others to define her, even though they probably looked down on her. She was a proud Black woman who walked and lived with purpose. She demanded that we act, speak, and approach others with a like attitude.

She began early on, instructing us that "You are God's child, let your light shine." Even though she and I would have confusing battles in my teen years about how Black and White people could or should interact, I remember her stance as being, "We belong here, they belong here, so act accordingly."

The lessons stuck. I never retaliated when I was the target of racial incidents, nor did I initiate. I didn't carry some of the baggage, the anger and bitterness, that I saw in others who were also scarred by those struggles early in life. Despite my confusion about my place in the world and my embarrassment about our being poor—or perhaps because of them—my lack of bitterness allowed me to build relationships with a wide range of people.

My mom's beliefs did not prevent her from being a realist. When I got together with friends from high school, I traveled to the White neighborhoods near Olney High to play ball and socialize. My mother often said things that let me know that she considered my safety to be at risk. From time to time, I would get probing questions from her, my uncles, or other concerned adults who became aware that I was spending lots of time in White neighborhoods where they feared that people or the police might not have my best interests at heart. My mom's questions about my White friends were aimed at assessing whether they really had my back. She made it clear that she expected to receive the dreaded "Hello, Mrs. Harris? I have some bad news about your son" phone call on some sorrowful night.

In my youthful naïveté, I brushed off her concerns and treated those conversations with measured skepticism. The divide between my mom and I grew, and I stopped sharing all but the most frightening details about my encounters. Of course, I know now that her fears and concerns were well founded and that things could easily have turned out differently. Race relations were tense in Philly. There were often threats from people I encountered—to me, my friends, or to the parents of friends I visited—but I usually tried to shake them off.

However, some threats were more troubling and required more serious consideration.

One such incident occurred on a summer night in 1973. As the proud new owner of a 1965 Chevy Bel Air sedan (I had saved up and bought that oil-burning red beauty of a car for $500), I had even more freedom in moving about the city. I had arranged to see a movie with my friend Stephen, a close connection from high school. After parking on the street in front of his house, I went up to ring the bell and was greeted by his mom. His sister and I were classmates, and I knew the family well. We talked for about twenty minutes and then Stephen and I departed for the movie. Some moments after we left, his mother got an alarming phone call from a neighbor. An angry voice screamed into the phone, "If that 'N-word' ever comes to your house again, you won't have to worry about having a house. We'll break every window and burn your house down!" (An interesting and potentially unwise threat on a block of row homes!)

On our return to the house at midnight, Stephen's mother met us in the street and directed us around to the back where she frantically explained about the phone call. She recounted the message tearfully and told me that while she still wanted Stephen and me to be friends, she needed me not to come to the house again. Out of respect for them and with a renewed awareness of the consequences, from that day on I picked Stephen up three or four blocks away from his house whenever we met to go out.

Other friendships at this time suffered from similar incidents, as White parents of girls I knew called each other to discuss the "Reggie problem." ("He's a nice kid, but do we really want him dating or marrying our daughters?")

These experiences were deeply hurtful and wounded me emotionally for years. And there were thousands of them. Each time I had an experience like this, I was made to feel less than. I felt that the sky was lowered over my head. From my personal experiences, school lessons, books, magazines, movies, and the all-White TV programs that played on our TV, I got the message loud and clear: All is not available to you. Get used to it.

And yet, something in me could not consent to that. I didn't want to accept that my presence was a problem. I developed an early desire, born of my own need and longing, to heal my own hurts and work to make myself feel whole. One way to do that was to make others feel good, to affirm them and gain their trust. My goal was to make contact and friendship with anyone with whom I could begin to set the world right. Looking back, I see that in my desire to overcome my own personal powerlessness, I found solace and purpose in trying to shift the paradigm.

I didn't know at the time how heavy the weight of accumulated slights and rejections would grow to be, nor the full emotional toll of my efforts to be a bridge builder and to set the world right. I didn't speak about these internal tensions to anyone, and I did my best to bury my feelings of pain, confusion, and dismay until I sought counseling and race relations training later in life.

My experiences of trying to span the great divide between the races showed me just how wide that chasm is. Welcome to the world of bridge building in America, Reggie Harris.

CHAPTER FOUR

A DETOUR, AND A TASTE OF FREEDOM

Even with my early positive musical experiences, a career as a musician almost didn't happen for me. Growing up in my fundamentalist Baptist home and church, I was on track to become either a minister or a missionary. I was being trained in my church to that purpose. During the years that I was singing in the church choirs, I started being recognized as a role model for other kids and eventually became a young deacon.

After being baptized at age seven, I had to endure being called on to offer prayers and testimonies in front of the whole church fairly regularly. It was novel to have a kid who could stand up and act like an adult in church functions. A few other kids and I would be asked, on the fly, to fashion a prayer for the congregation. We used a set of ingredients that still exist today as part of the fabric of Black church liturgy, passed down from the late 1700 and 1800s. I quickly learned the form for prayers:

1. Thank God for life, health, and sanity (no small thing given what we as a people have been through)
2. Praise God for all gifts and for being God (redundancy is encouraged)
3. Acknowledge the general unworthiness of humans (a constant theme)

4. Thank God for providing Jesus as the means of salvation (again, redundancy is encouraged)
5. Pray for specific things in the community and world (the list is fluid and up to the person)
6. Ask for things that will improve or solve issues (God is in control, but it is important to tell God what you need)
7. Acknowledge that life will end and ask for mercy when it does (time to wrap it up)
8. Close with a flourish (establish your signature but keep it real)
9. Amen (go sit down)

Even at that young age, I was cognizant of the elements of style and substance. I found that I could deliver a prayer on the spot that could stir the emotions of the people in the church. I was good at it, but I didn't really enjoy doing it. Or more accurately, I loved being complimented for the skill, but I didn't feel the deep, emotional passion that the words were trying to convey. That disconnect was hard for me to process as a child, so I tried to ignore it. I learned to give the people what they wanted, but the pressure was, at times, overwhelming. As an obedient kid, I saw no option for complaint.

I was also selected at various times to represent the church in a variety of youth groups and conferences. I was always expected to hang out with the adults, and though I was well liked by my peers, I'm sure that most of them considered me to be a goody two-shoes. As such, I was never invited to any parties or gatherings that the young people put together themselves.

By high school I was constantly hearing "You'll make a great minister someday," which was not at all what I thought I was suited to be. The problem was, I had no idea what I wanted to be. And since I was used to doing what was expected of me and did not like disappointing my elders, I made choices that I thought they would approve of rather than following my own desires.

I remember being at a conference in Pittsburgh in 1973 when the movie *Godspell* was released. There was a young man named James from another church in Philadelphia that I befriended on the first night, who asked if I wanted to cut out from the evening session for youth delegate leaders to go see the movie at a local theater. I didn't know about the movie but it sounded fascinating, so I said "Yes!"

As we prepared to leave the hotel, my youth leader Mr. Rhone saw us heading for the hotel exit and asked where I was going.

"There's this cool movie about Jesus and the disciples and we're going to see it," I blurted out excitedly.

"You're leaving the conference to go to a movie?"

"Yes, but it's one about the life of Jesus. It's new!"

"Reginald, you are here for a reason. The delegates meeting starts in thirty minutes and we're counting on you to be there. You're representing the church."

Of course, he had a point. The church had made my trip possible. But the majority of the conference attendees were on free time that evening. Anyone (or no one) could attend that meeting, and there would be another two days of conference after that. I didn't get to go to many movies as a result of our church policies, and this would feel like true freedom.

My new friend stood looking at me. He was missing the meeting too, but he had said this movie would be a big deal to see and that no one from his church registered a complaint. I stood with the two of them, torn between opportunity and responsibility.

Finally, I said, "I guess I'll stay," as my heart sank. I still remember the look on James' surprised face as he left. I went to the meeting, where nothing unusual, enlightening, or inspiring happened.

Godspell was magnificent—when I went to see it years later!

Having been nurtured and trained since I was five years old by members of my church who were convinced that I was minister or missionary material, after high school I attended a small Bible college in Atlanta to prepare myself for the ministry. It was true that I knew more about the Bible than most of my peers, could quote verses, knew all the books of the Bible in order, had taught Sunday school starting at age fifteen, and could even give sermons if needed. I was seen as an upstanding young man, and in most ways I was. But I had doubts.

I didn't know if I believed in the dogma of Christianity, and I was beginning to think that adherence to the strictures of evangelical teaching didn't feel right to me. I had heard other messages in my travels with my high school choir.

And there was a war in Vietnam that I had just missed getting pulled into because my draft number had been 362 out of a possible 366. Although I had no idea where the country even was, I knew that going over to fight there was probably not a good thing. The news and TV accounts were scary. (We learned later that young Black men were disproportionately called into war service in Vietnam, with Black soldiers making up 16.3 percent of those drafted and 23 percent of Vietnam combat troops, despite accounting for only roughly 11 percent of the civilian US population.)

Several of our church youth leaders had been called into the army, and none had returned in good shape. The most prominent of those was a sparklingly energetic and charismatic teen who came back to Philly a strange, distant, and confused shell of himself, and who was never able to resume leadership status. His subsequent marriage to one of the sweet, thoughtful girls of the church led to years of troubled outcomes for them and their kids. Prior to his leaving for Vietnam, I saw much of myself in him. When he returned, I thought, "If this is what happened to him, what would going over there do to me?"

I feared for what I didn't know and for what I might not live to become. But despite the unknowns, my church—and Black leaders in general—did what they always do. They supported the war and pledged us all as good soldiers. Black people have fought valiantly (and willingly) in every war that the US has been involved in since the revolution. It's been one of the key ways that individuals and BIPOC communities have tried to prove steadfast loyalty to this nation. Sadly, we have even fought with distinction in wars we were forced to sue the US government for the right to be included in, getting wounded and giving our lives in record numbers. Allegiance to military service and its sacrifice was and is still seen as an obligation to God and country in the Black community, even though discrimination and racism have robbed millions of Black people of opportunity, benefits, healthcare, and advancement in the distribution of the G.I. Bill and other veterans' rights.

My church did not teach me anything about that history or work to advocate for the civil or voting rights of our people. Those things, to me, should be a ministerial responsibility. My doubts about the church ranged from the creed to the evangelical religious practice to the political.

I'm not saying I don't appreciate growing up in the Nazarene Baptist Church, because there was a richness of faith and a resourceful intensity of the people that I still value highly. And I was steeped in the beautiful music of the church. Those early, life-affirming experiences I had at church grounded me in a cultural and community connection that still serves me on my personal and professional journeys. But I began to feel that a career and life in that church community was not right for me. There was a confusion growing inside that made me tense and unsure, though I became very good at hiding it behind an effective facade.

But off to seminary I went, 766 miles away, way below the Mason-Dixon Line, to prepare myself for the ministry. My mom took the first trip with me, and we went into the deep South by train. Along the way, we saw and experienced the last vestiges of Jim Crow, which were not completely surprising to us, having traveled to Virginia many times in the 1950s and 1960s to visit relatives. While we were able to sit where we wanted on the train out of Philly, the structures that had supported legal segregation (the separate bathrooms, seating, and dining areas) were still noticeable once we crossed the Mason-Dixon Line. There were a few remnants of "Colored" or "Whites Only" signs faintly stenciled on a wall or two. There were empty rooms off to the side in one station where we as Black folks would once have had to sit during our layover. In several places there were "extra" water fountain fixtures and benches in North Carolina and Georgia.

Mom stayed with me for a few days to help me get settled, and then after breakfast the third morning (where grits showed up unannounced on my plate for the first time) she got back on the train and left me to begin my year in the South.

The year that I spent in seminary in Atlanta, 1970 to 1971, was difficult, perplexing, and wonderful all at the same time. I was at odds with myself, at odds with the world, and at odds with so much of what I had been taught in church. But despite my misgivings about being in seminary and pursuing a career in the church, getting away from Philly and having time to think and stretch my brain was liberating. It gave me a taste of freedom and opened my mind and eyes to a much wider world. While I didn't fall into any of the circles of progressive thought that were rising in the city, I was suddenly able to create more space to make choices for myself. And the expanding landscape of integration in Atlanta contributed to keeping me from being harmed.

It was a graced year of discovery. I got out into the city whenever possible. I spent hours walking around Atlanta thinking and exploring. I interacted with people on the street, in stores, and with local guys on playgrounds while playing basketball. It was interesting to see the ways that people responded to me and to each other. There was more of a "How ya doin'?" vibe, even with strangers, than one would see or expect in the North. And people would invite you into their spaces, maybe even to their homes, in what is often described as Southern hospitality.

Though I was mandated by the college to go to church each Sunday and to live by a strict code of conduct, I broke rules wherever I could. I skipped church often for Sunday morning walks and found myself pushing against boundaries, challenging people or things that didn't seem right to me. I didn't go hog wild. But when I was expected to be inside, I took walks and went to movies. I was on a journey of discernment, wondering how I might become a more authentic me.

I coached a basketball team from a distressed housing project in the city, leading to winning a championship in a teen church league. (This entailed my first eye-opening encounter with kids on drugs when I observed three of my players sharing pills just before the start of a game.)

I went to NFL football and major league baseball games. I asked a few girls out on dates. Most of the girls I met at school were cautious and not ready to date a Northern boy who was seen as a wild seed, so I got used to doing things by myself and got comfortable keeping my own company. I raised my hand in classes (something I almost never did in high school), and I challenged teachers with questions and random thoughts. They did not appreciate being pushed, but since I was otherwise a thoughtful, engaging, and positive student, they usually took the challenges in stride with the idea that, with guidance, I would eventually accept their points of view. They were wrong. It only encouraged me to push harder, but with polite, renewed creativity.

After linking myself with a struggling but community-minded Black church, I finally found that my ideas about spirituality and service, while different than the evangelical beliefs I had been raised with, had merit. I came from a church and a neighborhood where the phrase "Go along to get along!" described both a religious and a life approach. This was akin to the notion championed by educator and national icon Booker T. Washington, that Black folk were not supposed to push too far or be overly aggressive in their demands or deportment. As children, were taught to stay in line and do as we were told by elders. My new authority figures in Atlanta fit right into that philosophy. We were counseled that in all things, we were to "Let go and let God."

In my new, evolving stance, I was quietly but firmly committed to choosing another path. I was looking to make my own way and find God on that path. That included, among other things, finding a church to attend in Atlanta that was not authorized by the school, just to see where it would lead. The church I found was more focused on social gospel and service to the community, in contrast to the focus on presenting an upstanding Christian image that had characterized my church in Philly.

And I discovered that I could support myself financially. I got a job after school at the family-owned Crown Candy Company. One night, after a few months there, I made an interesting connection with the president and owner of the company. We had brief conversations in his office, which I was responsible for cleaning, when he worked late. I found out more about Southern legacy and labor relations, and he discovered that I had a brain and wasn't just some Black kid who cleaned his office. As we talked, he discovered that I was from the North and was interested in finding out more about why I had come south. (His son was a student at the University of Pennsylvania.) It was a learning opportunity for both of us, and I got the feeling that he respected me in some strange, unequal way.

I was charged with cleaning the men's and women's restrooms every day, where I found out just how disgusting people can be in how they use such spaces. Day after day, I would come in at 4:00 p.m. to find that each gender had found a new level of low on how they could abuse their restroom space. At first it made me angry that people couldn't be more careful in using the clean room I had provided the night before. Later I came to realize that they were all doing mindless jobs, in a hot, oppressive, and in some cases dangerous work environment, while being harassed by management and paid low and insulting wages with little or no benefits. Why should they care about how they kept their surroundings? I pledged myself to clean it beyond clean as an exercise in service to them. Every now and again someone, usually one of the women, would say thanks. But for the most part, it was "same mess, another day." It taught me how to value my work even though others might not notice or care.

I also spent my time battling the White Southern foreman at that company, my boss, who tried to match wits with me over how the job should be done. I found easy and effective ways to complete my tasks in the allotted time by devising routines that differed from his preferred methods. That left me time to visit the chocolate room more often. (We were allowed to eat as much as we wanted but couldn't take anything out.) I hated how he skulked around, always trying to make life harder on a job that was simple but awful.

I was once asked a question about unions by one of the young women who worked there. She heard I was from the North and had heard from her sister in Minnesota that unions were a good thing. I knew very little (only what I gleaned from my mom who was in the union at her job as a seamstress) but I told her what I thought, and days later found myself in the foreman's office for a warning lecture about "unionizing."

The situation intensified one afternoon when that same foreman unjustly fired one of my seminary classmates, Adolphus, who was late getting to work for a legitimate reason. My other classmates and I had informed the foreman upon our arrival of the fact that he had been held after class by his professor. But when he arrived some twenty minutes later, he was senselessly fired. Adolphus, who we called Country Boy because he was from Sparta, Georgia, happened to be the hardest working person in our four-man cleaning crew. We advocated for him, and then I convinced our workforce to stage a labor action and then to quit in solidarity when the company refused to rehire our aggrieved friend. I scoured the area and found a job at a newly opened department store. I'm pretty certain that the Crown Candy Company never found anyone who cleaned those factory bathrooms as well as I did. I'm also pretty certain that business carried on. But we made our point.

During my year in Atlanta, I made a few interracial friendships in the still unpeeling socially segregated South. I also made myself a problem for the very evangelical administration and wore out my welcome at the college, which was wanting more of the boy who had arrived that September than of the wandering, boundary-pushing questioner I had become.

Mostly, I used the year to talk to anyone who could help me gain perspective on the world. I met a few wonderful people and had some marvelously freeing experiences that helped me heal from my confusion as I began to think for myself.

One of those people was an older Black man who was also a student at the seminary. Rumor had it that he had been in the Black Panthers for a time. His actual story was mysterious, and he never told me much about his path to being at the seminary or about his time in the Panthers. But from time to time, usually after one of my classroom challenges, he would pull me aside after class or somewhere on campus at night and say, "Hey, Young Brother. What was on your mind today?" as he'd ask me to explain what I was trying to do with the discussion in class. Typically, I had no real deep sense of purpose that impressed him. But he was always encouraging and would say, "You keep on thinking it out. You're making them nervous."

Another wonderful person I met, who became my best friend that year (and into subsequent future years) was Robert Elliott, seven days my junior and born right there in Atlanta. Robert, a tall Black man, was the son of a local minister in the area and part of a family of five kids. They were a close family that occasionally provided me with a home-cooked meal. Robert loved music, films, and TV with the same intensity that I did. Robert was whip smart and quick with language and had gone through the pains of being a young Black person in an integrating South. He was not a sports fan, but otherwise his general experience of life was similar to my own, raised to be a role model and targeted for leadership. We hit it off almost immediately. Robert was also a voracious reader, an acute observer and listener, and a willing partner in discussion.

We also shared the fact that both of us were at the school largely because our communities had plans for us. Robert gave me a safe place to talk about my frustrations and the fact that I lived with thoughts that were not particularly popular in the Black community. He had a Southern sensibility about him that made him seem more conservative, dutiful, and obedient.

He was not as ready at that time to challenge the forces that be as I was, but he definitely had his own thoughts about the ways that life should work. After several years in the military and working for the Georgia Department of Labor, Robert became more aware and outspoken. We've stayed in touch across the years and still have three or four conversations a year. I am extremely grateful for his friendship, and I know that I would have had a much tougher journey getting through that year without his insightful and engaging presence.

Another person who had a big impact on me during that year in Atlanta was a woman I fell in love (and lust) with. She was a nurse who was older than me and seemed very ready to settle down and marry. She was years above my experience zone, and my family back home wasn't happy about my relationship with her. They staged a distant but effective family intervention to derail it. At the end of the year, my mother summoned me home via a call from my Uncle Jimmy, letting me know that a plane ticket awaited me for immediate departure. While my nineteen-year-old ego felt betrayed by my family's intervention into my affairs in Atlanta, I was relieved to be released from the seminary. And some years later I would find reason to thank my family for slowing my rushing train.

CHAPTER FIVE

FINDING MY MUSICAL PATH

When I returned to Philadelphia after my year of seminary in Atlanta, I resumed my vocal studies with Mrs. Gatling and my place in the church choir. It was through that time of study with her that I had yet another defining experience. With her belief in my vocal skills, Mrs. Gatling suggested that I take an audition with a fledgling Black opera company that was starting up in Philadelphia. She apparently knew someone who was involved with the project, and within two weeks of my saying yes, she secured an audition for me in Center City Philadelphia with the director.

As familiar as I was with classical repertoire and having a number of pieces under my belt, I still knew nothing about opera and saw the opportunity as just one more thing to try. She helped me choose three pieces, and on the day of the audition I took public transportation into Center City and found myself outside of the address listed on my invitation.

I remember standing in front of that building for half an hour or more, telling myself to mount the stairs, open the door, and go inside. But I found myself unable to move off the sidewalk. It reminded me of my first year in high school when I stood outside of the orchestra teacher Mr. Maola's room for fifteen minutes, armed with a letter from my junior high teacher, unable to approach him to gain a place in his string section. On that day in front of the opera building, similar fears and feelings of self-doubt kept me paralyzed. Then, having missed the appointed time, I simply made my way back to the subway and went home. There would be no opera audition for me. That company went on to establish itself as a place for young Black classical talent to be nurtured without me ever sounding a note.

For years, I wondered what would have happened if I had managed to overcome my reticence and had gone in to sing for that audition. I don't remember what excuses I made to my mom or to Mrs. Gatling for having failed to follow through, or if they were upset, but it wasn't too long after that my lessons with Mrs. Gatling came to an end. With what I know now about the world of classical performance and how difficult it has been for people of color to find opportunities to excel—how stellar talents like Charles Williams, Todd Duncan, Leontyne Price, and many others had to go overseas to gain acclaim that eluded them in America—I am grateful that I did not expend energy on years of training and struggle on a genre for which I had no passion. I did have passion for the folk music that has become my home, and even though there have been years of struggle and fighting for acceptance, they involved singing material that speaks to my heart and soul.

Around the time of that audition, I learned to play guitar. I was twenty years old, and a girlfriend had challenged me to learn two chords.

A few years earlier in 1969, I'd heard James Taylor's song "Fire and Rain" on a late-night WIBG radio program called *Americana Panorama*. It was a seminal moment for me, a Black kid living in North Philly with wide-ranging musical tastes who was negotiating a mostly White high school landscape. The strains of Taylor's guitar and voice awakened something in me that I couldn't explain. Having heard that song, a path to a life in music and an actively engaged citizenship was begun. What opera didn't do for me, folk music did.

It would take years for that awakening to become a reality. That moment of hearing James Taylor's plaintive, crisp sound was enhanced and intensified as I became inspired by the music of Gordon Lightfoot, Aretha Franklin, Cat Stevens, Pete Seeger, Stevie Wonder, and countless others. I experimented with those myriad musical influences, and they stirred the juices of creativity in my body and brain. Murmurs of the spirituals and gospel songs of my youth simmered together with the classical and jazz compositions I had heard in school. I moved and swayed to the pop and rock classics that filled the airwaves. Together, all these musical influences set me on a different course than what was expected for a kid of my background. With a steady diet of faith-based music in my life, and with the strains of more ethnically based sounds bombarding me in the streets (and from my sister secretly playing a more Black-focused mix of Motown, R&B, and soul whenever my mom and grandmother weren't around), it was unlikely that I would choose to love and perform music that was so "White." My eclectic preferences would later bring challenges from family, neighborhood friends, and some audiences that I was "not Black enough." That accusation would take years to resolve in my head and heart.

Nonetheless, all around me there was a fusion of sound and message that lifted me into the ozone of boundless self-expression. Music, as it so often does, opened new windows of meaning for me and allowed me to test my wings in a new atmosphere of artistic freedom. And with joy, my life and career dreams took flight.

The seeds of my love of folk songs were sown in second grade, when Ms. Churn introduced us to the music of Woody Guthrie, Pete Seeger, and a young singer named Bob Dylan. How was I to know then that years later I would become friends with Pete and Toshi Seeger and Tom Paxton, and be inspired by the work of Bernice Johnson Reagon, Harry Belafonte, Phil Ochs, and James Taylor? That I would be traveling the world over, singing songs and telling stories in concert halls, at festivals, and to audiences of every background imaginable? It's been a journey down a twisting, less traveled road, one that still causes me to shake my head in wonder at times.

On that road, I have spent most of my musical life working in collaboration—in childhood singing with my mom and sister, and then in church and in school choirs. That desire for collaboration continued in my adult life as I discovered that music—my inspiration and my way to express all that I love and hope to represent—has been greatly enhanced by my connection with other musicians.

It has been both a privilege and one of the greatest blessings of my life to have had Kim Richards Harris as a musical and marriage partner for forty-two years. In 1974, while working as a camp counselor at College Settlement Camp north of Philadelphia, I met a young woman, Kim Richards, whose early life and musical experiences were strikingly similar to mine. We quickly became friends, sang night after night to the kids in my cabin and at campfires and, discovering that we would both be attending Temple University that fall, began spending lots of time together.

We spent hours every day singing on campus. We had both been in choirs and taken music lessons for years, so we knew the value of practice. During nightly song and guitar practice sessions, our friendship quickly became a musical and romantic partnership.

As newly energized kindred spirits, we began spending every spare hour rehearsing, going to concerts, building a song repertoire, talking about artistic habits, figuring out arrangements, and playing with the burgeoning idea that a music career, which neither of us had ever considered, could be a possibility for us. We were both driven to see what we could make of our passionate harmonic unity, and struck out to find places to perform around the Philadelphia area and eventually to places in New Jersey, New York, and beyond.

We picked out role models and began to dream of glory and fame. We began inhaling songs, scoured the newspapers for possible gigs, and soon found that we were a great team at scouting and adapting to the various requirements of becoming an act. We took turns calling venues, in order to share the possible rejections. And there were rejections. But there were also many opportunities offered by people who were intrigued by the very look and sound of us. We were unusual in that we were a Black couple playing folk music, and that got us some early attention. It would later present us with more challenges than we would desire.

We began paying our dues, playing in restaurants, coffeehouses, shopping malls, clubs, on street corners—wherever someone opened the door in the Philadelphia/South Jersey/

Delaware tri-state area. We did four-set nights, weddings, open stages, company picnics, church services, political rallies—any kind of space that promised us a chance to be heard or get paid.

The only places we wouldn't play were bars where the clientele was either too rough and rowdy or too racist. We once took an audition at a popular bar in downtown Philadelphia called J. C. Dobbs, where the bartender/manager said, "Folks, I like your stuff. You're really good, but I can't book you. You're way too wholesome and you might get killed in here!" And later that year, someone did! With his encouragement, we found safer venues to play.

We played music for hundreds of church services and weddings. We even gained fans with regular stints on the Roman Catholic mass sponsored by the Archdiocese of Philadelphia that was broadcast on local TV on Sunday mornings, much to the chagrin of my faithful Baptist mom.

In the late 1970s we spent two years performing as regulars at the very first comedy club in Philly, a place called Grandma Minnie's. Featured as musical relief on multi-artist shows with comedians like Jay Leno, Michael Keaton, and other future comedy and film stars, we got a nightly master class in stagecraft and audience engagement. It was a wild place to perform, especially on Wednesday evenings when an open stage format brought people who were willing to say or do *anything* to get a weekend spot. We earned a place as one of the regular weekend acts and worked for meager pay (if we got paid at all) and all the food we could eat. But we were in show biz. It was good training for future gigs where "exposure" would be the best offer. But as they say in the biz, "You can die from exposure!"

During this time, we were also building an area following with frequent appearances on local morning TV shows, guest appearances on Gene Shay's folk music radio program, and by giving out business cards to anyone and everyone who would take them. We enjoyed a good measure of success and began to get small tours to places outside of Philly, once playing a weekend gig at a college where we were paid $700. We thought we'd made the big time—$700 for two days of work. (Not too long after that, we heard about a famous performer who was paid $30,000 for a thirty-minute concert, and we realized that we still had a way to go before we could relax into fame and financial security.)

When we moved on from the bar and restaurant gigs and into coffeehouses, arts centers, and venues in small towns and large cities, we were happy to discover that people came expressly to hear the music. This made it necessary for us to learn to deliver concerts with good pacing, humor, and emotional context.

Our early concert sets were heavy with covers of James Taylor, Gordon Lightfoot, Joni Mitchell, Cat Stevens, and a wide mix of other favorites. As young writers, we enthusiastically began to sprinkle in the best of our fledgling original songs. (To keep venue owners who only wanted cover songs off our backs, we would sometimes claim that a song of ours was a deep track from an album by one of the more famous artists.) Our approach helped us develop a style that quickly gained wide appeal with area audiences, while enabling us to assess reactions to our original songs. We learned how to command a room and not just suffer the indignity of being ignored as background music.

As our musical connection and success blossomed, we decided to marry in November 1976. Our union forged a partnership that became the successful international touring duo Kim and Reggie Harris. Our travels took us around the world for over forty years, entertaining audiences of all ages and backgrounds at over 300 concert performances per year. In 1990, we were invited to become John F. Kennedy Center Arts in Education artists, as expert contributors to the knowledge of the Underground Railroad and the music of the modern civil[3] and human rights movements. (Kim and I had done extensive research on the Underground Railroad early in our musical partnership, as I describe in a later chapter.) We were also recruited as scholars in the Council of Independent Colleges lecture program and became sought after as leaders in interfaith and ecumenical worship and practice.

To anyone watching our progress, we probably looked fearless and carefree. But in retrospect, it took the both of us to persevere, because we were always breaking new ground. We were integrating the market everywhere, seldom playing for Black audiences. And while we were good at winning over mostly White crowds with our smiles, engaging sound, and couple chatter, we always knew we were on display. As one of the only Black acts in a rotating list of area folk musicians, we were an anomaly—two energetic, eclectic, Black singer/guitarists doing music that wasn't what most Black people sang or

---

3   I often refer to the "modern civil rights movement" to indicate that this was a continuation of the movements for freedom from slavery that had taken place since the beginning of Black folks' (or "colored people's"—we were not referred to as African Americans yet) time in this country. As part of that struggle, they used song to focus hearts and minds, to gather the community, and to lay out their concerns both in the movement and outside of it.

listened to. Our increasingly intricate harmonies and arrangements were a mix of pop, folk, gospel, classical—a unique blend of crossover long before Tracy Chapman or India Arie made their splashes on the scene. It was both exciting and difficult, and would get harder over time.

Folk music was a world in which we would for years feel like imposters, waiting in fear for someone to say, "Wait a minute! How the hell did they let *you* in here?" Folk music was not a popular medium for Black people as performers at that time, unless you were doing blues or other music that would later be called roots. Most of those Black blues artists were older folks who were part of the famous folk revival—people who had been "discovered" by younger White artists down in the South and brought out to festivals and folk clubs for White audiences to experience as authentic practitioners of the music of struggle, such as Bessie Jones and the Georgia Sea Island Singers, songwriter Elizabeth Cotton, and blues and gospel great Reverend Gary Davis. We, born much later in the North, had not come from struggle in the classic sense, so had no claim to that authenticity.

We almost never ran into another person our age who was Black who owned an acoustic guitar or sang the types of songs we did. (I found out later that there were a few other Black folk musicians coming along as we were, making their way through that same web of challenge with some networking and hustle.) By keeping our ears to the wind and endlessly poking into any space we could find, we were signed to a company that marketed musical greeting cards. We recorded three or four that were sold nationally featuring our original songs. Initially, they sold well. But we later found out that company representatives began getting calls from suppliers in different parts of the nation inquiring if we were Black or White. It seems that many customers, with no photos included in the packaging, wanted to know what race we were. Something in our voices or our inflections signaled that there was an added element to us that they wanted defined. Apparently, sales decreased in some parts of the country once they knew. As much as we didn't want to face the facts, it quickly became apparent that race would be an issue in our career in many ways. We tried to deny it, but it just wouldn't go away.

Most of our colleagues were White and not at all aware or willing to believe that race was causing such a challenge in our path. Their lack of familiarity with the racial issues we were navigating led them to try to normalize the difficult feelings, comments, and challenges we were encountering or explain them away using a context they understood.

So many of our difficult racialized experiences came decades before the term White privilege was in the public consciousness. All traveling artists have stories from on the road. But most of ours differ from our White colleagues and friends, who blend in more than we ever have. In recent years, that's been one way I can make the point of what White privilege is all about. Back then, when I would share with friends some of the troubling incidents and experiences I'd had, I initially didn't know what to accept or reject in their explanations. It made me feel even more misunderstood and miserable, and I would doubt my perceptions and myself.

It helped that Kim and I were trying to tackle it together. And it was a relief when occasionally one of our Black friends or connections could provide a helpful reality check: "Nope, that ain't hardly right! No way!" Having had a momentary sense of being heard, seen, and understood, we'd move on again through the maze of racialized American experiences to the next oasis or trouble spot down the road.

The challenges we faced in touring the country as Black musicians made it necessary to keep our wits about us at all times and never let our guard down. It proved to be an exhausting endeavor. Days and weeks of traveling in places where there were no people of color was consistently stressful. It required us both to heighten our coping skills in order to get through each day. We also had to remember not to take that stress out on each other. That was not always an easy thing to keep under control, and I'm sure our relationship suffered as a result.

In this landscape of being a Black musician traveling in mostly White spaces, I often found myself feeling very lonely for not having close contacts in my family who could have made useful suggestions about choices I faced or provided informed emotional support. I did not—and still have not—shared many of my circumstances and feelings with members of my family in detail. My personal and career journey of coming to grips with race in America has been mostly an interior experience, shared only in specific moments for specific reasons.

In one sense, my family members know how hard it has been to navigate the terrain that has landed me where I am. They are African Americans who have had their own battles to fight and obstacles to overcome. For most of them, older and more seasoned, the journey was a far more difficult and dangerous one than my own, given the times they lived through.

Whenever the subject of overcoming racism comes up among Black folks, we often just go to the shorthand of "Yeah, well, you know how *that* is." It's a brief statement that encompasses decades of frustration and struggle.

In addition to feelings of loneliness and separation, I was acutely aware of the lack of family resources or access to prepared paths of achievement that is so often the plight of Black family life in America. Systemic racism has made it almost impossible for Black families to accrue wealth or pass down even the simplest societal gains or financial capital to their children.

Many of my White colleagues had parents or relatives who could loan or provide money, resources, connections, or advice to smooth their way into the start of a career. That was not true for all, but I am still in awe of the number of my White colleagues who came into a little money or land when a parent or relative died, providing a chance to advance a project and their career.

There was no established route and no financial support for me to become an entertainer, least of all a Black folk singer. Kim's mom was very helpful to us in our early days by giving us money for our first sound system and allowing us to move in with her for a year so that we could save up to buy better guitars. The comments I heard most frequently from my family were "Oh, that's very nice what you're doing, we're proud of you," "Good for you. I saw you on TV!" and "You making any money doing that yet?" One other favorite remark that was said more than once was, "Those White people really seem to like you. They treating you okay?"

Well, yes, yes and . . . no.

When Kim and I met at ages twenty-two and seventeen, despite having grown up in different areas of the city, we shared a vision of the world that looked, in one sense, limitless in hope and full of possibility. At the same time, we quickly became aware that being African American performers in the predominantly White world of folk music would be a lonely path of extended challenges to racial and societal norms.

As self-represented artists, we would often have to absorb weird and insulting conversations over the phone, or in person at conferences, as sponsors awkwardly informed us of their intentions to either book us or not based on their perspectives on race or what they thought their audiences would take. When asked why they were hesitant to book us, student or staff representatives at colleges would say, "I like your music, but we don't have many Blacks on our campus." The college students would continue, "Well, you are really good! Maybe we can take your materials back for the Black Student Union members. They're not here but we can give it to them." (We knew to cross that gig off the list!)

When we finally managed to get connected to some agents, we would warn them that race would be an issue in booking us. They were always incredulous at first but would soon discover—much to their chagrin and anger—that it was true.

The exception to this was Black History Month, when we got gigs *because* we were Black. Once colleges and schools discovered the need to present programming for Black History Month, it was possible for us to work every day of the month of February, with two engagements some days. (We'd play a "nooner" and then some nearby school concert in the evening.) We would be booked and advertised on a campus as a "Special Black History Celebration" as part of the college's "commitment to diversity programming." In truth, we were most often one of the only acts of color to play that venue that year. And we would find out on arrival that those gigs often came with extra duties that our White colleagues said that they didn't encounter.

And come March first, it might be time to go home.

Looking for summer gigs, we found that many folk and acoustic music festivals were much the same, with most having only one or two acts of people of color on a festival roster, while they booked twenty to forty (or more) White artists—mostly White men. Very seldom did we ever get booked at the same festival as one of our Black colleagues—as if we all did the same thing. One of the enduring jokes among artists of color is that if more than one of us is booked at a festival, we suddenly need to wear our name tags. We have all gotten used to being mistaken for each other and have simply learned to say "thank you" when being complimented for a good performance by one of our peers.

When we began getting booked to perform at colleges and universities, which helped us in our quest to make a living as touring musicians, a downside was that we suddenly found ourselves traveling to places where being a minority was a much bigger deal. First off, many college campuses are located in rural or fairly remote areas. We were often in places where very few Black folks lived, if any. The journey to the gig, finding food, stopping to ask directions, or looking to get our car serviced in the days before GPS and online apps led to interesting or uncomfortable experiences with townsfolk.

"Not from around here?"

"Oh no, we're here to do a concert at the college."

The looks we sometimes got would stop a bear. Of course,

there was also a time or two when we got invited to some stranger's house for dinner.

If people of color did live in the area, it might be unusual for them to be on campus unless they were an employee or a suspected trespasser looking for trouble. Once on campus, there would be more looks and random questions to determine our status: "Can I help you?" asked in a suspicious tone from someone who these days would be known as a "Karen."

Seeing another Black face on a campus or in a town of mostly White folks led to the development of a code between Kim and me. One of us would say, "Oh, there's somebody we know!" to alert the other to the presence of a person of color in the area. It was a pressure release. And if a POC did pass you while walking, it would be likely that you would get the head nod of acknowledgement. It's an established cultural statement and moment of connection to show respect via a nod or smile. Most often, Black people who are operating in an all-White or mostly White world will choose to acknowledge another person of color when they encounter one. However, it's also a reality that the stresses of racially isolated situations may make a Black person reluctant to break their "cover" to greet another Black person, which can disrupt that feeling of community connection.

If Black folks came to our show, they might take the opportunity to regale us with cautionary tales from their personal experiences in which things got dicey on or off campus. "Be very careful 'round here!" There was a lot to think about.

Stopping at a local business or a bank to cash our check after the concert could take up to an hour, just to override the questions from well-meaning but suspicious faces. "We don't often get people from the East Coast here." Since we were usually one of a very few, or the only, performers of color to grace the campus that year, each of these encounters, good and bad, would put us on notice that we were once again representing the race. So we had to be on our best behavior to make certain there would be another gig down the road. We definitely found ourselves navigating a deeper level of racialized America than we were used to on the East Coast. (This is discussed more in chapter 10, "Touring While Black.")

I realized early on that the nonstop stress of having to account for race in the process of booking, traveling, and performing was affecting our career success and was taking a toll on my physical and emotional health. Despite having been exposed to racism and prejudice for years, this burden still came as a shock to me. My mental attitude had been honed by years of being told "If you work hard, be diligent, and nice, you'll eventually reach your goal." That mantra, and its cousin "You can be anything you put your mind to be," died a slow and agonizing death, as the level of acceptance and access we longed for proved to be complicated and elusive for many years.

After too many unsatisfying episodes of being singled out as "special" performers in demeaning ways, we decided to get some antiracism and oppression-reduction training at the National Coalition Building Institute. Kim and I also began to do research in history and education that would allow us to address the issues of racism and prejudice as part of our concert performances at colleges, art centers, and in schools. After many years of being buffeted about by both overt and covert racism, we made a choice to respond by trying to educate and address the issues with music and focused programs.

To get support for these efforts, we joined several activist and artistic groups such as Folk Alliance International, Local 1000 (the traveling musicians union), the People's Music Network, Clearwater Inc., the Children's Music Network, the Black American Music Association, and other groups that have used art to highlight instances of injustice. Those affiliations and our growing connection to the education department at the John F. Kennedy Center for the Performing Arts in Washington, D.C., led to more opportunities to educate people of all ages and backgrounds about the issues of racial inequity.

By creating shows like "Music and the Underground Railroad" and "Dream Alive: A Celebration of Black History" and being part of events that taught about the modern civil rights movement, we became valued resource performers. Our work countered the national misconception that Black people were simply passive recipients of the benefits of the "American Dream" or an underclass of former slaves, workers, and violence-prone malcontents. Our music and performances showcased the rich fabric of achievement, sacrifice, loyalty, and ingenuity that Black people have contributed to our country despite constant waves of brutal discrimination enforced both legally and illegally in American society.

CHAPTER SIX

A WAY OUTTA NO WAY

The synergistic connection between Kim and me gave both of us physical and emotional support in the tense reality of integrating the world of folk music. For forty-two years, we hitched our star-filled dreams and passions to each other and pulled that heavy wagon of uncertainty together. During those years, we helped each other grow as we honed our musical skills, sharpened our perspectives, and became seasoned advocates for the power of song. Through lots of practice sessions, performances, and pushing ourselves to try new material, we became better musicians. We supported each other as the contours of racism pressed in on us. We triumphed, suffered, and sacrificed as we grew into a brand that most knew simply as Kim and Reggie.

There were musicians and community friends such as Grammy winners Cathy Fink and Marcy Marxer, Grammy nominee and activist John McCutcheon, college lecturers Barry Drake and Pat Padla, local concert promoters and activists Bruce and Linda Pollack-Johnson, and many others who recommended and booked us for gigs and gave us helpful advice about venues, equipment, and promoting ourselves. But they couldn't offer much advice in countering the many doors that were closed to us because we were Black.

We began connecting with fellow performers of color like Josh White Jr., Reverend Robert Jones, and others with whom we could compare notes or just share some nourishing moments of commiseration. It was only through the gracious welcome and encouragement of these friends and some more famous White folks that over time we realized that we not only belonged but had at last found a home.

We had several champions who loved us for who we were and booked us repeatedly. There were people like Susie Erenrich, a social movement history documentarian who produced concerts with various members of the civil rights movement leadership, and members of the People's Music Network for Songs of Freedom and Struggle, who saw the connection in what we were doing to justice work even before we knew how to make it. They gave us a chance to join concerts and introduced us to other social movement elders like James Forman, Julian Bond, Matt and Marshall Jones, and Hollis Watkins.

Philadelphia volunteers Barbara Smith and Jeannette Yanks of the Philadelphia Folksong Society's Odyssey of Folk Music program enabled us to do community events and hatch our school program on the Underground Railroad. Dave Fry, the artistic director at the Godfrey Daniels club in Bethlehem, Pennsylvania, booked us to open for songwriters like Bill Staines, Eric Andersen, and others, giving us a lift into the small concert venue world. Performing at Godfrey Daniels gave us our chance to perform in a real folk club, which introduced us to new audiences and led to a cycle of growth in our talent and careers. We used those gigs to watch how the seasoned "road dogs" (nationally touring performers) worked the room, and it helped us to hone our pace and patter.

As I mentioned, one of the biggest champions of ours in Philadelphia was the dean of folk music radio, Gene Shay, who introduced us to a wide radio audience by having us play on his Sunday evening folk show numerous times.

We met a local music promoter named Joyce Brown whose club, the Blushing Zebra, featured more overtly political artists. On one of her shows, we met and befriended Pete Seeger, who was the headliner. That night, before we had met, I almost stepped on Pete's banjo, which he had left haphazardly sitting on the floor behind the curtain. He was seated nearby, writing. Noticing that I had just missed his banjo, he looked up.

"Who are you?" Pete asked.

"I'm Reggie Harris, one of the performers tonight."

He extended a hand. "I'm Pete Seeger." I thought to myself, "I know who *you* are!"

Later, he and his wife Toshi gathered all the performers together and asked, "How shall we do this evening?" and invited us to help make a set list. I remember thinking, "Wow! How thoughtful is that? They're famous and they still seem to care what we think."

That would not be the last time they would demonstrate the art of being inclusive and gracious. Pete and Toshi soon started having us perform with Pete at festivals and concerts. They included us as part of a diversity concert at the 2005 General Assembly of the Unitarian Universalist Association in Fort Worth, Texas. Their influence and support later made our playing the Great Hudson River Revival possible, and with that we became part of the larger Clearwater Revival family of artists and environmental activists.

Pete and Toshi made it clear that we were there to share

our truth, tell our stories, and sing in our voices. The faith and trust that they gave us to represent our people in our unique way was liberating and inspiring, and it continued until Pete's death in 2014. Pete was only a phone call away when we needed some star power to raise money or awareness for a cause.

Pete, who regularly traveled into the South during the hotbed days of the civil rights movement, was always at the forefront of finding ways to include Black and other performers of color into the mix wherever he could. It was Pete who was on stage the night in August 1964 when the bodies of civil rights martyrs Andrew Goodman, Mickey Schwerner, and James Chaney were found buried in an earthen dam nearby in Meridian, Mississippi. Beloved for being a thoughtful ally for justice, Pete was asked by some of the local folks to announce the news to the gathered crowd. After delivering the solemn news, he led the crowd in singing a song. Pete was known for being a respectful guest in those Southern communities, showing that he understood his privilege and tried to use his fame and presence to benefit the communities he was there to serve.

The same was true of other White performers like Peter, Paul, and Mary; Joan Baez; and Phil Ochs, who came into those violence-scarred environs to show solidarity. They often brought curious news crews with them that made it easier to publicize events that White audiences or media might pass up if it was "just Black people." They stood as allies alongside Black artists like Harry Belafonte, the Freedom Singers, Odetta, Josh White Jr., Matt and Marshall Jones, and Len Chandler, as well as with local singers, activists, and civil rights workers, to raise songs and bring the public's attention to the cause. I have greatly admired those remarkable role models for showing up to support important social struggles without becoming the center of the story.

It was in meeting Matt Jones and Len Chandler that I first saw up close Black men who played and sang like me. They had far more scarring, dangerous, and demeaning encounters with the music and political worlds than my own. Matt was field secretary for the Student Nonviolent Coordinating Committee (SNCC) and had been arrested and jailed for protesting injustice twenty-nine times. These men validated for me that racism and prejudice were issues that had to be faced and taken on. Matt and his brother Marshall became my friends and mentors whose example I could learn from and follow. They had truly faced the valley of the shadow of death and survived.

One of the people who became a conduit to information and access for us was Sonny Ochs, the sister of songwriter Phil Ochs. We met Sonny at a folk music event in Philly, where she introduced us to Phil's songs. We became fast friends, and she became one of our most devoted advocates. She invited us to perform at many of the Phil Ochs Song Nights she presents around the country, which have worked to keep his music and message at the forefront of political activity.

Phil wrote about issues of race, prejudice, and social change, and his songs have influenced my songwriting in powerful ways. Phil's music, and our inclusion in these concerts, energized our growing political stance and songwriting, and the musicians that we met were the kind of people we wanted to know.

Sonny introduced us and our music to new venues, festivals, and radio DJs such as Chicago's Rich Warren (longtime host of the Midnight Special on WFMT), Wanda Fischer at

WAMC in Albany, Mary Cliff in Washington, D.C., John Platt in New York City, Mike Regenstreif in Canada, and many more.

Along the way, we joined the National Association of Campus Activities, an organization that connects artists and agents to events at college and universities. They sponsored an annual conference at which over 1,000 college students and staff and several hundred performers, artists, and agents gathered to exchange information and negotiate bookings at colleges and universities for the next year.

At one of their conferences, I experienced a powerful moment of serendipity. It happened during twenty minutes of eloquence that turned into a driving motivation and profound breakthrough in my life and career. The speaker was the noted author, lecturer, and human rights activist James Baldwin, who was the featured speaker at the conference's opening night banquet. Dinner was part of the weekend package, so with the added incentive of a free meal, I sat with friends amid clinking glasses and dessert forks, waiting for his address to be over and for the evening to turn to more concrete opportunities. Mr. Baldwin was famous and indeed even controversial, but truth be told, I was more interested in maximizing our chances for earning a living.

Baldwin began his remarks to the students and college staff with comments about the importance of education. He then turned to address the artists in the room, most of us musicians, comedians, hypnotists, and various novelty acts. He said, "The role of the artist is to observe what happens in a society, and through your discipline and filters, show your society what it is that you see. That is a special and time-honored role." In that moment, I began to feel a sense of pride that he had singled out those of us who were artists as the most important people in the room.

"In your role as an artist you will often see things that are troubling—things that need to be fixed or need to be changed. Things that hurt or kill others. It is part of your responsibility to show those things, as well as those that make people feel good. Society will often not want to see these things, but it is your responsibility to show them anyway. They will not always love you for it, but that is your job."

I knew, in that moment, that something in my vision and life purpose was being challenged. I wasn't completely certain that I understood the meaning of his words, but I knew on some level that my life as an artist was going to change. It took years to implement those words into the work that I offer as part of my artistic vision, and I'm still working on it.

Through all these experiences, good and bad, Kim and I grew into our individual selves, and our marriage had to shift and change. Ultimately, after a hard and diligent process of rigorous soul-searching, discernment and dialogue, our marital and professional partnership came to an end in 2016. While we are still processing that major change in our lives, fortunately, with work and time, we have both moved on in fulfilling ways. Kim followed her lifelong interest in studying and teaching theology by earning a PhD in theology from Union Theological Seminary in New York City. She is now an assistant professor of theological studies at Loyola Marymount University in Los Angeles. I am now a solo touring artist and lecturer. We still perform together occasionally, with shared passion and purpose.

Our experiences have prepared us both for leadership in our new roles and for our reconfigured relationship as friends, colleagues, and ongoing collaborators. Kim and I continue to share a camaraderie and are still on a mission to assist each other when possible, using all that we've learned on this remarkable journey of life and hope. We are still partners in the mission of seeking justice and truth. We hold in our hearts a great amount of respect for each other, and I am proud that we have both been able to live into the values of love, honor, and respect that we spent so many years singing and talking about.

My mind and heart are full to overflowing with the experiences that took Kim and I from Philadelphia to just about every state in the union (forty-eight in total), across the ocean to Italy and Austria, England and Germany, and on the highways from Florida to Alaska, playing for audiences of two to 40,000.

I am blessed with a wealth of memorable moments. One of my favorites happened as we ended a concert with a gospel choir in a beautiful theater in Cologne, Germany, in 2018. Brought back onstage for a third encore, Kim and I stood side by side, leading an audience of 1,000 German music lovers in singing Pete Seeger's song "Rainbow Race." I was filled with a feeling of transcendent joy as I witnessed music overcoming barriers and uniting people, making change and trust possible. It is the same feeling I have when I lead an audience of children in song in schools across the United States. Music touches people in ways that transform lives and make our planet safer, saner, healthier, and more just. Listening to people's voices rise up, I know that the choice to make music the focus of my life was important not only for me, but for the world.

If this journey has taught me anything, it is that music will help heal the world if we share it with each other. This is the song in my heart; this is still my work in the world.

CHAPTER SEVEN

A CULTURAL AMBASSADOR FOR MUSIC, HEALING, AND HOPE

As I moved more deeply into my life as a musician and story-teller, I came to realize that I am a great-great-great grandchild in a long line of those who have been nurtured and chosen by my community to keep history and important messages alive using songs and stories. I am a servant of those who have prepared me—my teachers and mentors, my childhood church community—as well as of those who come seeking wisdom.

Initially, I resisted the role of being the voice of tradition and legacy. As a young person, I was not always interested in hearing stories about the past. Our family and community gatherings would often include old folks telling stories in a way that included a lot of laughing and reminiscing, which I found slightly interesting but tedious. But having been taught to be polite and respectful, I took the stories in. Fortunately, the scraps of story fabric fell into the cupboards of my active brain, where they sat until they could later be assembled into something whole. Years later, as my career as a musician and educator began to take a more definite shape, I began to recall those distant stories and pair them with information gained by my research, giving me useful material I could offer as a resource to others.

In sharing these stories, I serve as a modern-day griot. Traditional West African griots are sources of oral history: storytellers, praise singers, poets, and musicians who pass on information that promotes life-affirming interactions. In my ancestral cultural tradition, griots call people of all ages together into the village center to sing in harmony and to remind them of our shared existence. Uniting the old and the young lifts up good deeds and reduces the stressful or selfish actions that break us apart. I am a conduit in a long-accepted and valued way of helping people feel more joy and more meaning in life. As with griots of old, my chosen songs and stories focus on history and humanity.

So we sing . . .

> Ain't no harm to keepin' you mind . . . stayed on freedom.
> Ain't no harm to keepin' you mind . . . stayed on freedom.
> Ain't no harm to keepin' you mind . . . stayed on freedom.
> Hallelu . . . hallelu . . . Hallelujah!

Through my performances, I hope to add meaning, context, joy, truth, and substance to the community. I seek to share stories that illuminate both the harsh realities and challenges that so many of us face as well as the dreams and promise of our human connection. Sometimes the songs I write tell the stories of people who have created—or are trying to create—opportunities for positive change in the world, or they might highlight an issue or a cause. I want to offer people a way to engage, to invite them into a conversation that brings forth new ideas, new solutions, and hope for bringing them to fruition. Most importantly, I want my audiences to feel moved.

As Maya Angelou, one of our treasured elders, once related, "I've learned that people will forget what you said, people will forget what you did, but people will never forget how you made them feel."

My role as cultural ambassador extends to my online presence. On Facebook, Twitter, and Instagram, I seek to create chances for dialogue, inspiration, and unity. I navigate spaces of tension where just speaking or writing the phrase "Black Lives Matter" or mentioning White privilege has the capability for sending people into a simmering silence or defensive expression of frustration and fear. Since joining Facebook, I've used the platform both to network and to extend my ability to reach people who exist in different social, professional, and political bubbles than my own. I've had many breakthroughs there. People say, "You can't change minds on Facebook!" For the most part I agree with that sentiment, but there have been moments where a shift in attitude or thinking has occurred.

In one such case, a random White male responder on my very public Facebook page, went from writing the comment "Who cares what YOU think, CLOWN?" to eventually signing off with, "I wish you a good day, Sir." This evolution followed a fierce twelve-hour back-and-forth of online dialogue and article sharing that, at day's end, transformed his white-hot anger to a more respectful attitude that led to a discussion where we each saw the other as a thinking human being. It was more than worth the time spent. The fact is, every engagement with others on issues of race and justice, even on Facebook or Twitter, counts for something—maybe more than we know.

As a performer, I am most often presenting for audiences that are composed of people who don't look or perhaps even talk like me. In truth, I work mostly with and for people who don't share my social location, history, or culture—White folks. Hence my role as cultural ambassador.

Like most African American men, I've learned many skills that have enabled me to navigate and survive the tricky terrain of being Black in America. These skills include reading people, observing their behavior, dealing with oppression, coping with disappointment, code-switching (being able to shift linguistically and behaviorally between Black and White cultural norms), fronting (putting on a facade to impress people), keeping a low profile, smiling to reduce conflict, and engaging in "non-threatening behaviors" so as not to offend White people and to promote solidarity.

As a people, African Americans have often been forced to remain on the sidelines in community acceptance, power distribution, and equal access to institutions and social and financial capital. That there are still "firsts" being achieved by people of color in so many areas of the American experience is a hard reminder of how difficult the road has been. Ours is still very much a segregated society. The struggle that began with slavery has been absorbed into our bones and was set into a cultural frame by the sighs, whispers, and shouts of the spirituals and other songs we composed.

> Stony the road we trod, Bitter the chastening rod
> Felt in the days when hope unborn had died
> Yet with a steady beat, Have not our weary feet
> Come to the place for which our fathers sighed?

We have come over a way that with tears has been watered
We have come, treading our path through the blood of the
   slaughtered
   —James Weldon Johnson, "Lift Every Voice and Sing"

I am frequently asked how I, as an African American man, found my way into this mission in a nation that has had such a painful and intractable problem with racism and prejudice. The thought of crossing into such territory required deep thought and the commitment to interior personal work. It required developing patience and acquiring a level of knowledge, savvy, and skills that most people of color find too hard, too invasive, too exhausting, or simply not worth the effort.

But I felt called to this bridge-building work. I see several strands in my life that led me to this path. First, my family of origin story, which I address in the "Hickory Hill" chapter of this book, put me in the racial/cultural mix from the beginning. A conjugal master/slave union between a Black woman, Bibhanna, my great-great-great-grandmother, and her White owner's son, Williams Carter Wickham, forged a history between the White Wickhams and the Black Hewletts. I am of both lines in blood and historical legacy.

Second, I lived a childhood that had me integrating schools, youth groups, sports teams, and other social gatherings at a time when laws were changing and, to some degree, hearts were opening to the call of racial healing and diversity. I found myself having friends of all races and backgrounds and often had to absorb the tension in those groups to help move them to unity. Looking back, I guess it is not surprising that I was voted "Best Personality" in a high school class of over

1,000 students at a school where race riots had erupted two years earlier. I didn't campaign, I made friends.

Third, I have a deep passion for fairness and justice. Even in competition, I have a very strong desire to have justice and equality at center. When playing basketball games without a referee, I chose to call my own fouls. It just felt wrong to try to gain an unfair advantage, even if we lost.

Fourth, I grew up steeped in the culture and music of the Black Baptist Church, and those songs, hymns, stories, prayers, and parables are deeply embedded in me. They are the root from which my intercultural bridge-building grows. My early experiences of leading prayers and singing in the church choirs helped me develop the skills I use as a professional musician and ambassador—stage presence, a strong voice for singing and oratory, and the ability to be present in the moment, to captivate an audience, and, hopefully, to inspire them. I just share a different message.

The fifth strand that contributed to my evolution as a cultural ambassador is a set of experiences that caused profound shifts in my psyche. I've described the one initiated by James Baldwin's speech about the role of the artist. Another transformational experience came in 1994, when I found myself sitting in a circle of about twenty-five artists and activists in Providence, Rhode Island. We had answered the call of performer and storyteller Bill Harley, who with the assistance of his wife and manager Debbie Block had invited us to participate in a recording project sponsored by WGBH, the public radio station in Boston. The goal was to produce a CD of civil rights songs, old and new, that would eventually become the album *I'm Gonna Let It Shine: A Gathering of Voices for Freedom*. Some of the remarkable folks in that circle were former members of the original Student Nonviolent Coordinating Committee and the SNCC Freedom Singers, such as Chuck Neblett, Bettie Mae Fikes, Hollis Watkins, and Wazir Peacock.

Bill asked each of us to share why we had chosen to come. As we went around the circle, the answers took a familiar tone. Each person shared their thoughts on the importance of the songs and some platitudes about enlightenment or wishing for the success of the project. I was mentally preparing to offer something in that same spirit when the joyful spell of gratitude was shattered by Cordell Reagon, who issued a challenge. I don't claim to remember his exact words, but I certainly recall the intensity. It went something like this:

"I hear what y'all say. But I'm wondering, in the spirit of what these songs meant to us back in the day and what they mean now to the movement—for what these songs have kept alive and for the people who sang them as they were beaten, tortured, or killed—I wanna know, why are you really here?

"Are you here to get famous? Here to get your names known? Or are you here to put yourselves on the line to work for justice and to keep the legacy and power of these songs alive? I need to know why you're here before we start singing these songs!"

His words shocked me, and they silenced the room. My first thought was, "Wow, that's kind of rude, him second guessing all of us like that." But it got me thinking. I knew of Cordell, and I knew in a cursory way what all of the SNCC members had been through. Most of us had only read about the struggle. A few others in the room, such as Guy and Candy Carawan, had been there, too. (Guy, one of the chief song leaders of the movement, was responsible for teaching "We Shall Overcome" and other anthems to the SNCC students. He and Candy were on the spot as adult leaders when much of that history happened. They were White people who had cast their lot with Black people and who were also in the line of fire in Mississippi, Alabama, Georgia, and anywhere else that the movement went.)

Cordell was right to call us out. In my heart, I knew I was going to have to dig deeper. The answer would not fully come to me that night. It would grow slowly over the years as I had more contact with other elders who continued my education and added to my knowledge. I deepened my commitment to tell the stories and sing the songs.

On the last day of the recording project, my voice was spent from long hours and constant singing, and fatigue was creating lapses in my focus. I decided to sit out the planned recording of one last song, the gospelized version of "Up Above My Head," which was being led by Bettie Mae Fikes.

Bettie Mae, one of the truly incandescent voices of the movement, is civil rights royalty. She was born into a family of gospel singers and preachers, and from the time she was four years old she traveled with her parents' groups the SB Gospel Singers and the Pilgrim Four. Known as the Voice of Selma, she inspired folks throughout the South, joined SNCC at sixteen, worked with Bernard Lafayette and his wife on the Selma Project, and sang with Cordell, Hollis, and others in the Freedom Singers before moving to California. This was one of her signature songs.

But I was done. Exhausted. I went into the WGBH recording studio truck to listen to the group as the song went down. The signal was given to begin, and like a lightning strike, I heard the Voice of Selma, still rich and full after all these years, deliver that first line with a passion and a tone that sent shivers up my spine.

"*Up . . . above my head!*" The sound rang out from those speakers like the angel Gabriel's trumpet.

"Stop the tape," I almost screamed at the engineer. Startled, he did just that.

"What's wrong?" he asked.

I was using an authority that I didn't have. Bill had taken me into the truck several times during the week, so the engineer was aware that I was helping as a consultant, having produced a number of my own recordings by this time. But I was not in charge.

"Uh, nothing, actually," I stammered.

From the moment I heard her voice ring out, I knew where I needed to be, and it was not in the truck. As tired as my voice was, there was a spirit in that room where Bettie Mae Fikes was singing that I knew I needed to soak into my body.

"Tell them there was a glitch. Tell them you heard a noise. Tell them anything. I'm on my way!"

And we sang:

> Up above my head
> I hear music in the air
> And I really do believe
> There's a God somewhere

Over the years since then, I've made sure to be in "the room where it happens" as often as possible so that I could absorb knowledge from those leaders. Years later, it was with Guy and Candy at the Highlander Folk School; with Hollis at the 50th reunion of Mississippi Freedom Summer in Jackson, Mississippi; with Dr. Bernice Johnson Reagon in Washington, D.C.; with Pete Seeger at Riverside Church in New York City; with Andrew Young in Indiana; with Julian Bond in Maryland; with Odetta at the Clearwater Revival; and with Harry Belafonte at Lincoln Center Outdoors. At these performances, I've kept in mind what Sister Bernice counseled: "We're not here to sing pretty, trying for perfection. These songs carry the pain and the triumph of struggle. So you got to get some of that into your voice, so people hear it and know it's real."

My relationship with those elders slowly shifted my focus from dreams of fame to holding up the wisdom of the sages. And as people like Pete Seeger, Dr. Charles Blockson, Margaret Block, and others encouraged me, I embraced the mission to increase awareness of our nation's hidden history. And now I find that I am one of those elders.

Many of my role models for compassionate and justice-oriented activism came from those whose lives began as part of the oppressor group. As I came to understand the nature of racism, prejudice, and White privilege, I gained a deep appreciation for just how difficult it can be for a White person to see the systemic racial and cultural conditioning they've been subjected to, let alone change their attitudes and take actions to try to overcome it. Witnessing their ability to change and to work to put more love and justice in the world allowed me to affirm my own belief that all human beings have worth. Goodness and right are not owned by any one group.

I've now come to embrace the words of both James

Baldwin and Cordell Reagon as part of my being. I try to portray, through song and story, an honest depiction of the state of our union. And if, as Baldwin said, that honest depiction isn't pretty or appealing, my job is to find a way into that portrayal that others can comprehend and appreciate.

And when I sing the songs of the civil rights era, I sing them with the knowledge that the folks who created those songs knew that they had rights as citizens that were being denied. They knew that they were doing their best to treat everybody right and live in a spirit of equal justice for all. They believed, deep in their hearts, that the God of their faith, the same one that White folks also prayed to, talked about fairness and justice in the Bible. They figured that they would provide an example for those White folks who hadn't come around to tryin' fairness yet. They sang the songs and taught us to do likewise so that someday we could all overcome. I carry them with me as I go, with the hope that the message or emotion will touch hearts and minds and bring alive a feeling of understanding in others.

It has been a fascinating, challenging, and fulfilling task to find the right material, balance, pace, and language to share what I feel compelled to present, trying to reach people who are not of my background or culture. I have to walk a fine line between telling the truth of my people's history, which is often brutal and disturbing, and not alienating people. It's hard work, but it's a risk worth taking.

Experience has taught me that I must keep my ears and heart open, since every opportunity is different than the last. While I may plan to offer a certain set of songs and stories, the energy of each audience and my openness to receiving it always dictates what transpires.

As a cultural ambassador, it is my job to build bridges, to spread love and not hate. Sometimes this requires sublimating deeper feelings of anger and grief. It has been a journey filled with complexity. It is a role that I have taken on with joy, some fear, and a huge amount of respect and caution. But this is clearly what I was born to do.

My ancestors left me a collection of cultural gifts—resilience, persistence, hope, faith, and the ability to move among and make friends from different cultures. They also passed on the narratives, music, folk tales, visual art, and creative language that have influenced all aspects of American culture and life.

Like a set of comfortable hand-me-down clothes, these gifts are imbued with an awareness of the past. They offer protection from the harsh heat of hate and the icy cold winds of loneliness as I travel to places near and far. I sing to spread hope and the promise of a more just world. I use my cultural wisdom to join like-minded hearts of all races, colors, ethnicities, and backgrounds to find greater understanding and move beyond racism. That's worth waking up for.

CHAPTER EIGHT

"ARE THESE STORIES TRUE?"

"Are these stories true?"

The question came from a fourth grader who was seated at the back of the classroom. It was inspired by an age-appropriate but honest description of life in slavery. It's a question that I've heard many, many times. As always, I smiled, and then in as calm a voice as I could muster, I said, "Yes, these stories are all true. I know it's hard to believe. But you don't have to believe me. You can look them up."

For forty-plus years, I've been working as an artist educator in schools teaching students and educators about the Underground Railroad, the modern civil rights movement, and about how music informs and inspires our lives in the present day. This is work I love to do. While I get great joy traveling the world singing for adult audiences at house concerts, in concert halls, festivals, and in famous art centers, there is nothing like the magic of being in a school somewhere in America talking about issues that many adults think we should hide from kids. I love interacting with students during and after my program on the early anti-slavery movement called "Music and the Underground Railroad" or my presentation on the civil rights movement called "How Martin Climbed the Mountain." These dialogues provide the moments when I feel the most hope for the future of our world.

Kids are honest, open, curious, and more than happy to entertain themselves if you don't happen to be interesting—or if you seem like you're trying to hide something. Whether I'm telling a story to 200 kindergarten to third graders or I'm teaching the song "Wade in the Water" to the coolest, most disinterested-looking ninth-through-twelfth graders, my years of engaging with students from every region of the country has taught me that there's always a way in. The goal, and the challenge, is to discover the way in together. Music and story help students discover, engage, and then demonstrate their learning in ways that are not only fun but effective.

In pictures and letters that come through the mail weeks after a performance, students show that lessons on Harriet Tubman, Henry "Box" Brown, or the marching children of 1963 Birmingham have hit the mark. Teachers report that "the students are still singing those songs, and they've made connections to present-day students and events in Parkland, Florida; Tulsa, Oklahoma; and Columbine, Colorado." The connections between past and present become more than words on a page. One of my favorite pictures was drawn by a second-grade girl after an Underground Railroad program. She drew herself crying, with a thought bubble showing a girl in slavery. I love that drawing because it demonstrates the emotional impact of slavery, her understanding of injustice, and her ability to reflect on it.

To tell the truth, I never really liked going to school. Other than getting to see friends, making music, playing sports, and eating lunch, school was always a chore for me. I was a little too social, a bit too easily distracted, loved talking more than listening, had poor study habits, and as one of my teachers said, "Reginald, you are endlessly rambunctious!" From my earliest days, the main thing I loved about my time in school was the connection to other human beings and the chance to learn interesting things. Too often, what I was being taught seemed to have little or no actual relationship to the world around me. I loved it when my teachers found a way to make stories of social and historical events relevant in a way that captured my attention and showed me how that information connected to my life or would affect me in the future. In those moments, school made sense and was fun. That did not happen very often.

Just getting to school was a challenge for me. Getting up early (I am not a morning person), getting dressed and spending over an hour on public transportation, and getting into a seat on time was a chore unto itself. And once I got to school, there was not a lot going on to excite me about this time-consuming daily event that adults were so in love with. Almost none of what I studied had a connection to any historical events or accomplishments that involved people who looked like me, although I wouldn't notice that until years later. All of the notable figures and protagonists that we studied were White, aside from George Washington Carver and the repetitive mention of his facility and fascination with peanuts (he actually was quite the amazing scientist on all subjects agricultural and did so much more for farming than just peanut research) and a sporadic mention of Frederick Douglass every couple of years or so. My schooling from kindergarten to senior year of high school was virtually exclusive of any mention of anything done by, advanced by, or attributed to people of color.

My awareness of the lack of representation of people who looked like me was reinforced when I was about nine years old and had to make a trip to the emergency room at Temple University hospital to get stitches for a cut on my knee. Early in the evening on a summer night, I forgot not to slide on the pavement outside my house during a very energized game of running bases I was playing with my friends. I was safe but took a good slice out of my knee. After greeting my bloody-kneed self at the door, my mom hustled me off to the Temple University Hospital emergency room eight blocks away.

On entering the building, I remember looking up at a large, prominently displayed board with pictures of about twenty to thirty White men. Mom was in a hurry and, sensing my delay, squeezed my hand and pulled me along toward the registration desk. Later I asked her, "Who were all those people in the photos?" She said that they were the important people who helped to run the hospital. It registered with me that, just like in my school textbooks, in the newspapers, and on TV, it seemed that all the people who were important in the everyday world were White.

That small moment of visual imprinting left an impression that I still remember deeply all these years later. So much so that on a recent visit to a hospital in Ann Arbor, Michigan, when I came across a similar display board, I noted that while there were a few faces of color and some women on that particular display, the general look of the board was not tremendously different. We as a country still have work to do to make leadership roles more equitable and accessible so that all kids get to see people in roles of authority who look like them.

My general sense of history and culture, aside from what I

was getting in my neighborhood or at church, was that Black people were slaves for a time (without much information about how we got into that quagmire), and then there was the Civil War, and then World War I, World War II, and then Rosa Parks sat down on the bus. And since Rosa's insurrection was such a recent event—with me being born in 1952—that was still much too fresh and controversial a subject to discuss in a classroom.

It is still true that history is very often taught from a limited, Eurocentric perspective. Though we have made progress from those days of two-dimensional learning where only the accomplishments of Europeans and a few far distant people of color are recognized, we are still struggling to balance the frame with other racial, gender, and ethnic perspectives holding equal weight. That is why the work I do in education is important to me, and why I am motivated to spend so much energy to be a resource that expands students' knowledge and understanding.

In all honesty, my decision to become an educator was not initially triggered out of some magnanimous desire to reframe the painful learning experiences of my childhood or reform the education system. In fact, my becoming a musician and an educator happened more as a reaction to leaving the seminary in Atlanta. In 1971, after that rather confusing and emotionally wrenching first year of college, I returned home to Philadelphia without any sense of what I might do. I moved back in with my family and began searching for a job. My friend Jan Sprow (then Thompson) mentioned that she knew someone who might be able to give me a job working at a center for emotionally challenged kids. I landed a position as bus and classroom aide at KenCrest Centers, an organization that provides educational services to children and adults with developmental or intellectual disabilities.

It was a fascinating introduction into a world about which I knew nothing. I came to love the children and their families and the people who dedicated themselves to work with this population that had mostly escaped my purview. It wasn't that I didn't know families with children or adults who were developmentally or intellectually disabled. There were several in my neighborhood or church. But for the most part, in those years, such individuals were hidden away or ignored in general life.

I worked at the center for about two years, riding the bus morning and afternoon with a driver to pick up children from their homes and then working in the classrooms with teachers or on trips to various places around Philadelphia for educational enhancement. I was fascinated by the way the teachers and other staff were able to make progress patiently and skillfully with their students and with the ways these new skills and behaviors added value to the lives of the kids and their families.

My supervisor found out very quickly that I had musical talent that could be utilized in the classroom. Since song was a large part of the curriculum, I was often called on to sing or help the students learn songs. It was joyful yet difficult work that at times would overwhelm us with the obstacles these families had to overcome. My time there, however, provided a great window to the vast needs in the world of education.

After working there for about a year, I decided to try to become a teacher in the special education field and, encouraged by my supervisor, returned to school at Temple University, taking classes at night. My first class was an English composition course where the professor required us to write stories. Each class she would give us a different prompt, which we then had to turn into a story using elements of writing style. Suddenly, I discovered that I had a gift for story-craft and that I enjoyed creating tales, often personal in nature, for my classroom assignments. I can now track the start of my songwriting and storytelling career to that weekly exercise. In time, I would focus my attention more specifically on courses aiming toward becoming a secondary school English teacher.

Meanwhile, an energetic, new young teacher named Sharon came to work at KenCrest at the beginning of the summer. Sharon expanded my world by taking me to folk concerts at the Main Point (a very popular music venue just outside of Philly) and to other folk music gatherings. She eventually inspired me to purchase a guitar.

Having decided to return to school full time, I left Ken-Crest that June for a summer job at the College Settlement Camp, an overnight camp for children located just outside of Philadelphia with a great legacy of bringing kids together from different socioeconomic backgrounds and creating opportunities to expand their worlds. This was the camp where I met Kim. In addition to that fortuitous occurrence, my horizons were expanded along with the campers as I met counselors from around the country and the world, most of whom played the guitar. For me, it was a summer of free guitar lessons and exposure to folk songs as we watched over our kids.

When Kim and I embarked on our career in folk music, like struggling musicians everywhere, we were always on the lookout for opportunities to make just a few more dollars to pay our bills (and hopefully one day become rich and famous). One such opportunity came about when we joined the Philadelphia Folksong Society. Our goal was to eventually perform at the Philadelphia Folk Festival, a prestigious, long-standing icon in the world of festivals that had hosted many of the musicians we revered. That honor would eventually come our way after years of trying. As members of the Folksong Society, we were often called upon to perform at hospitals, nursing homes, and small community events where we would be paid as community service artists. Each performance provided a small stipend of about $25, which went a long way in lean months of just enough gigs.

We soon became featured performers in that series, which brought us to the attention of a woman named Barbara Smith. Barbara called us one evening to offer a new opportunity. She told us of a program called the Odyssey of Folk Music, which sent performers into schools for a week at a time to promote music of historical or cultural relevance. She offered us a place in that program if we could come up with a short offering that schools might be interested in.

We wracked our brains trying to figure what we could offer. During our discussions, Kim remembered a snippet from something she saw when she was in fifth grade. A performer had come to her school for an assembly program and mentioned that songs were used as codes on the Underground Railroad. He had demonstrated this by singing a song that she recognized from her church, "Let Us Break Bread Together on Our Knees." We did some research and found out that it was a song that was often used to call the slave community to a secret meeting, early in the morning, where they could worship and discuss important issues like trying to make an escape. Singing that song at night, often heard but not understood by the master or overseer, would allow the meeting to take place before the master was awake and aware. It was a song that was sung in my church as well.

With that small idea and a little more research, we put together a thirty-five-minute program, "Songs of the Underground Railroad," and got a whole week's worth of work. Better still, our curiosity was piqued, and we were off and running to find out what we could about the Underground Railroad. There was scant information at that time, as much of it was still being discovered in slave narratives that weren't available to the general public. But we gathered as much information as we could and soon had enough for a full program that we offered to schools and colleges around the nation.

The next year we were blessed to meet Dr. Charles Blockson at Temple University, one of the foremost authorities on the Underground Railroad, and through his encouragement we did more research and recorded our first album of songs on that theme. That vinyl album, *Music and the Underground Railroad*, would eventually get the attention of people at the Kennedy Center in Washington.

The Kennedy Center subsequently booked us in 1990 for one week of shows in their Terrace Theatre series for hundreds of school children from the Washington, D.C., area. Those shows led to an opportunity to present a teacher workshop for sixty teachers in a brand-new program that would eventually be called Changing Education through the Arts. The program, in which I still participate, has now expanded to all fifty states and is a resource for educators, arts centers, and parents.

My years of collaboration with expert colleagues at the Kennedy Center have increased my knowledge and honed my materials to make them more useful to educators in their efforts to reach their students using the arts. Along the way, through performances in schools and art centers all over the country both with Kim and as a solo artist, I developed the skills and techniques I now use to present these programs for students and educators in a way that is uniquely mine but tailored for them. Membership in that Kennedy Center collaboration also opened doors to opportunities for Kim and me to share our gifts as artists and educators around the country and throughout the world, far beyond anything we could have imagined.

My memories of my own experiences as a student, combined with my deep love of music, history, and human rights, motivate me to be an educator who makes learning more historically accurate, more intersectional, more inclusive, and most of all, more fun. I want teachers and students to engage my presentations with the attitude of "Something *great* is gonna happen here today!" And when I leave a school or auditorium, I want them to say, "Wow, now I get why this stuff matters to me!" I want for them what did not happen for me.

Once, while doing performances for the Detroit Institute of Art in schools in Michigan, Kim and I had two astoundingly different experiences in the same week. At the first, a middle school in Benton Harbor, Michigan, we encountered a surly school secretary who, upon our entering the school asked us, "What show?" She then reluctantly contacted the vice principal, who showed us to the performing space and allowed us time to set up, without much assistance or interaction. At the prescribed time for the show, we noticed that no students were entering the auditorium. Our liaison from the DIA went to the office to inquire as to why no announcement had been made. Within minutes, a terse announcement went out over the school intercom system demanding that teachers and students "get their butts down to the auditorium for the cultural program!" After some time, groups of unruly students begin filing into the auditorium and loudly took their seats. Next to them were teachers with papers in hand looking very irritated about having had to leave their classrooms.

The principal arrived and, after minutes of boisterously trying to command attention, gave a half-hearted announcement that "this program sent by the Detroit Institute of Arts is a cultural enrichment that will make Black history relevant to all the students. Pay attention and try to learn something." With that, he left the stage, and we began our performance to rising levels of student conversations and little focus on the program we were beginning to present.

Over the years, we had developed a number of audience management techniques that, in most cases, allowed us to find the right level of engagement to complete the program. This has been true in schools from the most expensive and well-resourced private academies to the most under-resourced schools in the nation. In this school, however, with the teachers completely and utterly tuned out to what was happening, after a short time our liaison, respectful of our effort, walked out on stage and asked us to stop. She proceeded to announce that the level of disrespect showed by students and staff had demonstrated that this particular school was not interested in being enriched, thanked the students who had been paying attention, and announced that the DIA would be sending no more programs there until such behavior was addressed. We were in the van and on our way in thirty minutes.

That very same week, we were scheduled to perform at a Catholic school near Detroit that was run by nuns who, despite all of the changes in liturgical and Catholic circles, were still wearing full habits. Upon entering the office, we were greeted warmly and graciously and were shown into an auditorium that had seen better days but was still well maintained. One of the nuns showed us the meager sound system and, upon our assurance that we had our own, asked if she might use our microphone to get the students' attention when it was time for the program to begin. With that, she left us to set up.

After setting up our sound and multimedia equipment, we retired backstage to put on our costumes for our Underground Railroad show. We were sitting quietly talking to Angela, our liaison, when we realized that it was just about time for the show to begin. At that moment, the nun who had left us to set up popped back behind the curtain and asked again if she could use the microphone to quiet the students. We assured her that was fine and that the microphone was live. She left us sitting backstage and went in front of the curtain and began speaking an introduction.

"Students, may I have your attention!"

The three of us looked at each other in puzzlement, wondering if she perhaps was practicing her introduction. We poked our heads out from the wings and realized, startled, that 300 elementary school children had come into the auditorium and taken their seats without us hearing them do so. They were all seated in their uniforms, hands in laps, looking expectantly at the nun who was now describing what they would see in the morning's program.

To say that they were an attentive audience would not begin to come close to describing the way they absorbed our every word and action. It did not make them the best singing or participating audience, but it was clear that there was a high expectation for learning and observing in that school.

Each school community presents different opportunities for engagement and levels of challenge to overcome. This variety kept us on our toes and ready to react in the moment to what each day might bring.

As Kim and I began to find traction in getting hired for school performances around the nation, our travels began to take us farther afield and into areas that we had previously purposely avoided. That meant getting opportunities to tour in the South, a place that we both had fears and concerns about taking our shows (and our faces).

We were unsure how our message would be received, being two Black Northern musicians who didn't necessarily fit into the roles that Black folks could be expected to fill, namely blues, rhythm, or rock musicians. We didn't know if doing shows in areas like Duplin County, North Carolina, would be more than we could handle. However, the director of the Duplin County Arts Council, Merle Creech, called our agent and was so joyfully attracted to our program on the Underground Railroad that we couldn't say no. She told us on arrival that while we would be a shock for some, she was looking forward to people catching our energy and our positivity. And she said that we'd be among the first Black performers to perform in some of the area schools. Our time would be spent traveling between schools that catered to rural students, either mostly Black or mostly White, with Native American families also in the mix. She reminded us that we were very talented and personable and had her confidence.

For the first time in our career, we found ourselves playing in isolated rural and wooded areas out in the country in the real South. Each community was completely segregated: first Black, then White. In each case, we shared our message in song and story that the conductors and agents of the Underground Railroad, abolitionists of diverse backgrounds, had helped defeat injustice. Stories about Harriet Tubman, Thomas Garrett, John Brown, and the ordinary people who were heroes and sheroes of history brought home the important fact that people's hearts were open to helping others because they believed in freedom.

It was a rich week of greeting wide-eyed students and teachers hungry for this information and for our music. They clearly found this Black folk-singing couple from the North fascinating. And as always, songs opened the door to some fascinating lessons and discussions. We had many opportunities for modeling unity and seeing each other as human, leaning into the spaces that song creates.

It was an eye-opening week for us as well, as our fears about the South were eased by actual contact. At the end of the week, the Arts Council sponsored us in a concert that was designed to bring the disparate factions and races of the area together. I'll never forget watching as Black and White folks entered the space that evening nervously, then sat down in the church pews in a town that one of the local leaders described as being "betwixt and between the race groups."

Connected by songs, our patter, and encouragement from the stories, as the evening unfolded the audience united their voices as one. They sang with passion. Merle reported back to us that this was the first time such a gathering between the usually segregated groups had ever happened in that county. For us, it was the beginning of many more such evenings and was an opening to the mission of bridge building through music that is now an everyday challenge and joy.

Having performed in forty-eight states, in city, suburban, and rural settings, to student and adult audiences of just about every background one might imagine, including prisons and reform schools, I have now reached a point in my career where I feel comfortable creating an atmosphere of collaborative engagement, active participation, and joyful learning wherever I am privileged to find the opportunity. While I may have to ask a student or two to "get up and move to a place where you will not be such a distraction to your neighbors" from time to time, or rely on a teacher to corral a student whose behavior is making our efforts to write a song or explore the motivations of Underground Railroad conductors more difficult in the classroom, my commitment to make learning more fun for the students than it was for me usually rewards me with bright and open faces that are ready to take a journey back in time to see why those people were interesting and what they might have to say to us today. I feel fortunate that my experience has given me the tools to present myself in a way that gains the teachers' respect and students' confidence that this interaction will be worth their time.

On some days I'm arriving with the janitor at 7:00 a.m. to set up for back-to-back performances for a few hundred to a thousand students. On others, I'm doing an after-school workshop for educators or an interview. And on yet others, I'm leaving a college building after a lecture presentation at 10:00 at night. All of it makes me feel grateful, vibrant, and alive.

I know that I've been the recipient of great mentoring and modeling from more than a few history and education angels who opened up their vaults of wisdom to let me see the light that now shines brighter than a thousand suns. My educator and artist friends have shown me how to use music, drama, the spoken word, creative writing, visual arts, dance, and technology to engage students in ways that bring curricular connections alive and foster critical thinking.

Perhaps even more importantly, integrating the arts into education brings learning into a heightened mental and emotional space in our students, helping them to become more empathetic, humane, and justice-oriented citizens of the world. Arts education touches the whole human being—something much needed in our current societal landscape of misinformation, technology, and highly charged political divisiveness.

If we are interested in making the world a better, safer, more inclusive, and just place, we can bring that about with learning opportunities that are made more accessible by the arts. The arts engage people viscerally, and engaged people are happier people. Happier people make better decisions, get along with their neighbors, and, if given a good set of values, are more thoughtful and relational in the world. I like to think of it as the "engaged hope and joy factor."

My work of over forty years with the Kennedy Center and a variety of other educational and historical entities has led me on a profound journey of personal discovery and accomplishment. It has helped me to become a better human being. So when people ask me where I get my joy and where I find hope, I can honestly say that one of the most consistent places is in my work helping students see how fascinating history, and our connection to it, can be. To have a chance to create a historical framework and help students celebrate themselves as history makers is the best of all possible worlds.

Day after day, week after week, I have the opportunity to get up in front of an audience and say, "The Underground Railroad was not a train. It was people. People like you and me. People who believed in freedom and justice and decided that even though they were not famous, they could do something to change the world."

And every time I do it, I can see in the eyes of every student in the room that little boy who was me in Grover Cleveland Elementary School in Philadelphia, who sat hoping that today would be a fun day at school.

CHAPTER NINE

O SAY, CAN YOU SEE?

Our national anthem begins with the words: "O, say can you see by the dawn's early light / What so proudly we hailed at the twilight's last gleaming?" The lyric was penned during a battle in 1814, a contest of wills between the young country America—a team of rookies—and an established veteran competitor, Great Britain. The writer, Francis Scott Key, used the melody of an old drinking song to chronicle this battle for dominance.

"The Star-Spangled Banner" was approved for use during the raising and lowering of the flag by the US Navy in 1889, and in 1931 it was designated the national anthem. It received this designation despite having been written by a slaveholder who used language that referred disdainfully to the Black soldiers in slavery who fought with the British in the hope of finding their own freedom. Those controversial lyrics in the mostly unknown third stanza still raise the eyebrows and ire of many Americans when they encounter them today.

After some mild opposition to its inclusion at sporting events, the song held on and found use as an opening ritual at the 1918 Baseball World Series and in the nascent National Football League. The practice was quickly adopted by other major sports leagues. The tradition remains a staple in American sports today, and hence we are accustomed to hearing it sung before many games, tournaments, and sporting events. Sometimes it is rendered simply as a solemn, respectful moment, honoring the sacrifice of veterans and others killed in the line of duty. Sometimes it is inflated into a more outlandish spectacle, framed by militaristic bombast that includes fireworks, flags, cannons, marching bands, and jets flying overhead. It is supposed to evoke pride in being a citizen of the United States of America, the supposed "land of the free and the home of the brave," while also paying tribute to the quest for achievement and glory in competition.

Because the singing of the national anthem is a public musical moment that is part of the theater of sport, there is typically a selection process used to find a person worthy of the honor of singing the anthem. This often arbitrary decision-making process leads to a wide range of participants, with both exceptional and dreadful results. Most notable on the high side are renditions by artists such as Whitney Houston, Beyoncé, Lady Gaga, and opera star Renée Fleming, whose musical choices left audiences breathless. And on the low side? I'll just choose to leave them where they sank.

I've been one of those players waiting for the singing to end so that my teammates and I can engage in the thrill of the game itself, lost in thought about our game plan and wondering if we'll be at our best as players and teammates during the contest. I've also been a coach, watching my players and wondering what the team would do with all the information and drills we spent hours honing in practice. And I've been the person singing into the microphone, raising my voice to sing a song that soars into the stratosphere as the athletes nervously twitch and people in the stands wonder, "Did he start the song too high? Will he be able to hit that last note?" In all cases, I've come to appreciate the moment for what it is at its best—joyful, inspirational, and motivating.

I've had the privilege of performing the anthem at the start of basketball games in high school gyms with a few hundred people and in large stadiums before crowds of 18,000 to 40,000 fans. I've sung it many times for the Middleburgh girls basketball team during my years coaching them in my adopted hometown in upstate New York, with neighbors and friends singing along. I've sung it for the World Champion Chicago Bulls and the Philadelphia 76ers in a packed Chicago stadium, standing a mere twenty feet from Michael Jordan, Scottie Pippen, and my friend, Coach Phil Jackson, during the Bulls' run to a fourth championship in the National Basketball Association. (There is a video on YouTube of me singing the national anthem with David Roth at this Chicago Bulls game, if you're interested.) I've sung it at Citizens Bank Park for my hometown Philadelphia Phillies, one of the oldest franchises in baseball (and, unfortunately, one of the most losing teams in that hallowed sport). I've sung it solo and with others, by day and by night, in sickness and in health. In all, I have probably sung it fifty or sixty times at athletic events in many cities, and it has never lost its charm and thrill. I would be happy, though, if a new song were chosen for our national anthem, one that is inclusive and honors all of our people as well as our beautiful natural landscape. Jean Rohe's song "Arise! Arise!" would be a good candidate.

When it comes time for the game, the prescribed ritual usually begins with an announcement by a stentorian-voiced announcer who solemnly intones the introduction with a reverberating echo: "And now (*now . . . now*) . . . ladies and gentlemen (*men . . . men*) . . . I ask you to rise (*rise . . . rise*) . . ."—as those in the stands fumble with whatever it is that they are holding, eating, or drinking—"as national recording artist Reggie Harris comes to honor our country with the singing (*ing . . . ing*) . . . of our national anthem!"

Despite what this ritual has come to represent politically and socially, I admit that I still get the chills from it. As an athlete, coach, fan, and musician, I've been on all sides of that moment. As a spectator and a participant, I can attest to its drama and appeal.

I've talked at some length in this book about the many ways that music has nurtured, enlivened, and informed my life, from my formative early years to my present experiences. There isn't a day that goes by where a song, rhythm, or melody isn't resonating through my body. But right up against that backdrop of song and sound is my love of sports. I've spent most of my life reveling in that passionate realm of physical expression—a willing warrior of the fields and hardwood courts.

In my elementary school years, it was the joy of simple games like jump rope, wall ball, stick ball, running bases, catch, and backyard golf, which was played with a small rubber ball and a stick to putt the ball across the concrete into a drain. Our house was large but had only a small backyard, and I was always trying to escape it so that I could play with my friends out on 17th street. I always had to ask Nana, "Can I go play out front?" because we lived on a very busy street, and it took years to build up my grandmother's confidence that I could be trusted not to run out into the street chasing a ball or toy. Whenever I was allowed to play out in front of my house, I would joyfully play catch, ride bikes, and run foot races up and down the block, imitating favorite sports heroes or imagining future appearances in the Olympics. Every now and then, we'd trudge the mile up to one of the local playgrounds which provided us with additional open spaces for baseball or football.

When I wasn't granted that access, I played in my backyard or in the basement. In those early years, I did what kids did in those days—played thousands of games all by myself, to the imaginary sound of an audience screaming and cheering in my head.

In junior high school I was introduced to organized sports—basketball, box ball (a stripped-down version of baseball using your hand instead of a bat), and football—the game that would become my primary love for years to come. I began to discover that sports could create situations where I could experience deep personal relationships across racial lines. In recent history, sports have been one of the key places where players of all races have learned to work and play together and find common ground. The NFL, the NBA, and certainly Major League baseball (with the complicated lessons of Jackie Robinson and others) have served as places that challenged myths and negative racial attitudes. These leagues have helped people of different backgrounds to build trust, bolstered by the ethic of everyone doing their job and depending on others to do theirs. This was true to a certain extent in school sports too. However, after our success at playing well with others on our sports teams in school, we would each return to our segregated homes at day's end. Who knows what parents and students were saying in dinner table conversations about "what happened at school today?"

I wanted to join the track team, but unfortunately my mother couldn't afford to buy me track shoes in time for try-outs. This was one of many instances where her meager seamstress salary precluded access to opportunities.

I remember being thoroughly devoid of the skills needed to play football when it was announced in seventh grade that our class section would need to organize a team to compete against the other seventh grade sections. Most of the boys in my class seemed to already have developed those skills, and if not for a young Latino classmate who took pity on me and spent days teaching me to run patterns and catch with confidence, I might never have found a place as one of the contributors to our league championship.

We were crowned champions of the seventh-grade football league at the end of that fall season, but I don't remember anyone singing the national anthem as we were awarded our trophy. I do remember that I caught the winning touchdown on a play that had been suggested by my faithful friend. In the heat of the final game, he told our two star players that I would be the best one to throw to because, "They won't expect us to throw to Reggie. They think he stinks!" (I had caught only one pass in the game to that point.) I remember Louis Ballas (a White boy who was our star quarterback) looking at Hanford (a Black kid who was his best friend and our star everything else) and then both of them looking back at me. They almost simultaneously said, "You'd better catch it, or we'll kill you!" And as you can see, I'm still here!

Seventh-grade intramural sports were instrumental in building my confidence and taught me the value of working hard to master a skill. By eighth grade, I had worked hard enough to be a consistent player and became a team leader and more popular in class. By ninth grade and high school, I was a good enough athlete to compete alongside just about anyone and hold my own. I never made any of my high school teams but played intramural sports for all four years. My high school career was spent deeply engaged in musical activities (singing in four choirs) that left little time for advancing my athletic skills. I don't regret the decision to focus on music, as I made choices to prioritize my passions. But in the years after high school, I still had a driving enthusiasm for baseball and basketball, and that interest would keep me actively playing both sports for much of my adult life.

I grew up dreaming about becoming a major league baseball player. In my fantasies, I would be the centerfielder for the Philadelphia Phillies. I imagined playing on the same fields where Willie Mays, Hank Aaron, Juan Marichal, Ferguson Jenkins, Lou Brock, Dick Allen, and, of course, Jackie Robinson had played. I was aware of baseball's great experiment (and the book by the same name) that landed the first African American into the modern major leagues. Mr. Robinson's years of facing hate and resistance would have squashed most other players. He was a great role model for all, and as it turned out, he became a special one for me in the years after high school.

When I returned to Philadelphia from Atlanta after my first year of college, I helped organize and train a basketball team of high school kids from my church. The congregation sponsored them in a city-wide church basketball league. This advanced my connection to the game from playing to coaching.

At this time I also played on softball teams made up of former friends from high school, and that eventually led to me to join a softball league that featured all White teams from the Feltonville and Frankford sections of Philly. These were guys I thought I knew, and I didn't give much thought to what playing ball with them against a wide range of segregated teams would mean. I soon learned that at those games, both home and away, I would be on the receiving end of some nasty name-calling and threats. On more than one occasion I was subjected to less than humane treatment, as kids from the neighborhood threw rocks and pieces of glass at me while I played my position in right field.

The season of 1975 was my own lesson in breaking the color line. To my great dismay, some of the guys on my team, who had known me for years, turned out to be just as intolerant. I thought they'd have my back as my teammates and friends, but they often just laughed off the issues when I spoke up about them. On two occasions, two of my own teammates slipped one day and used the N-word during a team discussion while I was taking batting practice. It was a highly charged moment that left me drained, even as one player said, "Oh, Reggie, I didn't mean you." During my final year in the league, I couldn't figure out why I had gone from being an excellent fielder with a consistently high batting average to an error-prone "ground out" and nervous wreck. At the end of that season, I left that team and league without so much as a goodbye to most of those guys. It was a bitter experience to endure and an even more bitter lesson to swallow, one that took years to leave behind.

Reading books like *Crash*, a memoir written by former Phillies first baseman Richie Allen, and homerun king Hank

Aaron's autobiography *I Had a Hammer* gave me a new universe of respect for all the Black and Latino professional sports players who had to endure much worse, on a much greater level, from fans, team officials, sports writers, and others, for decades.

> Oh, say does that Star-Spangled Banner yet wave
> O'er the land of the free and the home of the brave?

Years later, I was thinking about my experience as the only Black player in the softball league with my high school friends as Kim and I stood on the field at Citizens Bank Park in Philadelphia, waiting to be part of the opening game ritual for a major league contest between the Philadelphia Phillies and the Toronto Blue Jays. The occasion was the annual anniversary game celebrating Jackie Robinson's entry into the major leagues in 1947. My friend John Flynn, the official troubadour of the Phillies, had arranged to have us sing on this very special night. On a night billed as "Faith and Family Night" that celebrated the memory of Jackie's outstanding contribution to baseball and the world, a sold-out crowd had gathered to welcome not only the current baseball teams but also a number of surviving Tuskegee Airmen, the Black heroes of World War II, and former players from the old Negro Leagues where Jackie Robinson himself had played before his triumphant debut with the Brooklyn Dodgers in 1947.

It was a night to remember as we sat in a green room under the stadium talking with those amazing men. Though no longer in game or flight shape, they were still full of pride and grace as they recalled stories and answered our questions about their experiences in baseball and in war. Their proud voices and laughter shook the room. To a man, they displayed a stature that spoke volumes about their bravery then and now. Then we were all led to the field to do our jobs, where we would salute them during the pregame ceremony.

On that night, there were six gospel choirs from Philadelphia strategically positioned all around the stadium to perform a pregame concert and then, together, sing the US national anthem in a stunning arrangement. Kim and I had been asked to sing the Canadian national anthem honoring the Toronto-based Blue Jays. As we stood on that field watching the youthful ball players on each team, I realized that I was as close as I would ever come to savoring major league baseball glory. I stood marveling at the grace of those fluid athletes as they ended their warm-ups, and then watched them as they looked with wide-eyed excitement at the Airmen and the Negro Leaguers. Their smiles showed such respect for the men who had paved the way for them to play this game and for those who risked their lives for our country. Black men whose lives required courage, determination, commitment, and bravery beyond anything we might ever know.

We stood in front of the third base dugout and began our performance. It felt ironic that the song we sang, "O Canada," was not one honoring our own native land. But we experienced that beautiful moment of synergy as a celebration of pride, determination, and human achievement that transcended national borders and personal dreams. It was a song of hope, and our voices filled that stadium with notes from our hearts meant to speak to the thousands in the stands and across the world on TV.

O Canada! Our home and native land!
True patriot love in all of us command.

God keep our land glorious and free!
O Canada, we stand on guard for thee.

At song's end, the crowd roared its approval. As we left the field, the players smiled, waved, and yelled, "Good job!" "Way to go!" "Nice singin'!" and readied themselves to take the field. We headed back into the tunnel to say our last goodbyes to those brave elders who had stood up for freedom and justice so many years ago. In that moment, as years and scuttled childhood dreams melted away, I felt just as good as if I'd hit a triple down the third-base line driving in three runs. I'd gone from running bases on 17th street to the major leagues . . . on a song.

CHAPTER TEN

TOURING WHILE BLACK

When Kim and I began touring across the country, we quickly learned that there are lots of places in America where Black faces are not seen and heard very often, if at all. This not only made our race a damaging factor in getting hired and affected audience attendance at our shows but also made touring very challenging. The simple, everyday interactions of life on the road were quite stressful in the days before chain restaurants and hotels were plentiful in America. At times our travels were just a few steps removed from needing a copy of the *Green Book*—the travel guide for Black folks published from 1936–1967 during the era of segregation—while trying to eat or find lodging without incident. Many of the slights we encountered were subtle or unintendedly awkward comments and actions by people who meant well, but many were not.

Our experiences in dining establishments ranged from having our entrance silence the ongoing conversations and focus all eyes on us, to awkward greetings by staff, to being ignored, to being seated away from all other diners. Our well-practiced routine for how we entered these establishments and conducted ourselves included entering with a smile and using our best manners. And we always left generous tips. Even so, we sometimes had bad experiences, as happened one summer day at a Denny's restaurant in Maine. We went for a late lunch and were left waiting at the front area unserved for fifteen minutes. On bringing this to the attention of the manager, we found ourselves seated at a table far away from all other customers, close to the bathroom. On protesting our placement, we were moved again, across the restaurant (to the stares of all in the building) to a more central table, wondering why we felt so on display. After the meal we sat in the car and questioned each other, deciding finally to make a call to the national hotline to lodge a complaint. It was better than the night that I cut my tongue on a shard of broken plate that was buried in my pasta, but not by much. In both cases, an apology was offered, but we did not return to those establishments when revisiting the area.

After a number of unpleasant experiences, we began to be more careful in our choices. If we didn't have a recommendation from a local person or a listing in a road food book, we would pick places near main roads, in main parts of town, and at intersections or well-traveled places with large windows where we could see inside before entering. We also chose, when possible, to sit where we could see our car outside. We learned to avoid places with an abundance of trucks and took notice of the presence of gun racks or confederate flags and symbols. We never put political or racial slogan stickers on our car. We experienced quite a few incidents while getting gas or seeking a meal in a diner that made us fearful for our lives and wary as we made our way across the nation.

We heard stories about other Black travelers having to engage in confrontations, fights, gun play, or late-night car chases by locals or some KKK group. We were often performing in small, out-of-the-way towns and cities and were lucky that more painful or dangerous incidents didn't occur for us. We were ever aware that we were a long way from home in a small town and that no one knew where we were.

Traveling 70,000 miles a year by car across the nation also made incredibly real a danger that we learned to fear back in Philly: Driving While Black.

One memorable incident happened early one beautiful Sunday morning when we were on our way home to Philly under blue skies on a clear New Jersey Turnpike. It was about 6:00 a.m., with no other cars on the road, when an unmarked car with flashing lights suddenly pulled us over. In fact, I wasn't even driving. Our new, candy apple red Ford van was being driven by our White, blond-haired keyboard player Conrad, and Kim was sleeping in the back.

After approaching on the passenger side where I was seated, the uniformed New Jersey State Trooper immediately directed me to get out of the car. Our verbal exchange escalated quickly, with him refusing to answer my polite, well-rehearsed questions trying to ascertain why he pulled us over. When I asked him for the third time, he put his hand on his holster and said, "You looked at me funny back there." I realized that this was the car I saw entering the highway a few miles back. I had glanced at it and our eyes met. Seeing nothing unusual, I looked away and went back to napping.

I reiterated that I wasn't the one driving the car and had been sitting in the passenger seat. To neutralize a very scary conversation, I got out and put my hands on the hood of the car as he instructed, fearful that he might actually pull the gun. Kim challenged him and got his badge number. He never addressed Conrad, and he abruptly left. We never got a response from New Jersey after our complaint.

I was once stopped by a policeman for Running While Black in a White neighborhood in New Orleans (where we were staying with a friend) by cops who "wondered why I was running," even though I was wearing running shorts and a tank top. I explained carefully that it was part of my physical conditioning routine, but they didn't relax until I gave the name of my White host friend, told them I was a visiting artist there to perform in New Orleans public schools, and offered the names of my sponsors. I stopped running in that area. Ahmaud Arbery wasn't as lucky while running in Georgia in 2020.

One year before Ahmaud was murdered, I was traveling solo from Rochester to Friendship, New York, following a concert at Nazareth College. I got on the road early in the afternoon and found that the best route to my destination was to travel on two-lane roads that run north/south through rural counties. At first I was mesmerized by the scenery, which took me through some gorgeous forestland and secluded farmland. Country road driving can be so much more relaxing and interesting than the more sterile highway scenes. But those roads are also less predictable and more potentially hazardous when Driving While Black.

About an hour into the trip, an old gray pickup truck pulled up behind me and began to tailgate me for about two miles. I could see two white men in the cab as driver and passenger. A little annoyed, I slowed way down, figuring that the driver would pass and be on his way. Even with my slowing to well under the speed limit, he refused to pass and instead slowed and drifted back for about a mile and then cruised up to tailgate again. We repeated this process a few times, and then he settled in at a reasonable distance and I figured our battle of wills was over. I set my cruise control and drove on enjoying the scenery. After about an hour, I noticed that, despite having made a number of turns in the road, the truck was still following at a distance. Every now and then he would close the distance as he had before, and after I slowed to allow him to pass, he would drift back as he had before.

This went on for another hour, several more turns, and finally, down to the major highway that would take me to my destination at Mt. Iraneus, a Franciscan retreat center started by my friend, Father Dan Riley. The retreat center is in a very remote location, and I was worried that once off the highway I would again be on unpopulated roads. I thought about trying to find a police station, but I knew that those in rural areas are generally unmanned outposts and was afraid that stopping would give these men an opportunity to do God-knows-what and speed away.

Now more than a little worried, I called a friend and talked through several possible strategies and made a plan. After covering about twenty-five miles on the highway, I came to the Friendship exit and, watching them in my mirror, exited the ramp. They followed me off, again staying at a distance, which gave me the chance to employ my strategy. I stopped at a stop sign, deciding not to act in any abnormal or panicked way, and then drove the two miles through a small town at normal speed. I knew that I would be making a right turn just after passing through town and then making another quick turn, leading to a five mile zone with lots of curves where I could accelerate quickly to put distance between us. As I made the second turn I hit the gas, rocketing the car up to 70 mph, hitting the curves quickly and watching for them in my mirror. I saw them make the first turn, but now I was flying! If I was successful, I would reach the turnoff for my road without them catching up and seeing me turn. After that, I'd be on several dirt roads and would disappear up a hill and out of sight. Fortunately, it had rained recently so hitting the dirt road kicked up no dust. (I remembered civil rights veteran Hollis Watkins talking about being grateful for dry dirt roads that made it harder for the KKK to get at the SNCC field workers during a chase. But I was grateful for no dust that day.)

Reaching my turn, I was off down the road and pretty sure I had not been seen. While I have no real evidence of their intent, it feels entirely suspect that a nondescript old truck would travel from just south of Rochester to Friendship, New York, on a random Wednesday afternoon in November, following an unrelated vehicle the whole way. In the same way, I've been followed by the police in Massachusetts, Missouri, Wisconsin, Indiana, and many other states for minutes or miles at a time. Sometimes they eventually stopped me, sometimes not.

Of course, I didn't have to be on tour to be stopped by the police for Driving While Black. In Philadelphia, as I got older, being stopped and questioned by police became a very normal thing. These encounters would happen regardless of what I might be doing or where I might be headed. My choice was to do what they asked, making myself available for a search and answering their questions, or risk being detained or worse. Particularly feared were cops from the highway patrol, a specialized division of the Philadelphia police. They wore tight uniforms and smaller stylized hats. Every encounter I had with them was unpleasant.

I remember one such encounter on Thanksgiving Day around 1971 or so. I was on my way to the family dinner at my Aunt Sweetsie's home in West Philly and I was driving my used Chevy Bel Air sedan, which I had purchased months before with money I earned from working at KenCrest.

I was running a bit late for dinner when I noticed the flashing lights in my mirror. My brother-in-law was in the car with me, and we both knew the drill. After pulling over, we sat quietly, my license and registration at the ready on the dashboard. Through my rolled down window, I heard, "Get out of the car."

I got out. There was a White highway cop on my side and a Black cop standing behind the vehicle at the rear passenger panel. "Both of you!" barked the officer on my side. My brother-in-law also got out, and we stood waiting for the next instruction.

The Black cop stepped toward my brother-in-law and said "We're looking for somebody. You might be them."

"We're not," I offered as I gave my license to the cop on my side.

"How do we know that? You look like them."

I don't remember what I said next, but my brother-in-law, a youth minister at a church in Baltimore said nothing. He was from Philly and knew better.

"Open the trunk" was the next order. I knew that I had constitutional rights that stated I didn't have to comply, but I also knew that not doing so would make us late and would possibly ramp things up beyond what we wanted to deal with.

My hesitation led the Black cop to say, "We can do this easy or it can be hard."

I opened the trunk. They looked in. Then they turned without a word, walked to their car, and drove away. We looked at each other, sighed in relief, and drove to dinner. Just another day of Driving While Black in Philly.

In the years I coached an all-Black basketball team in a church league in North Philly, I learned to tell my players to report thirty minutes earlier than scheduled so that there would be time for a car filled with "too many Black teens" to be stopped, searched, and released first. It was a strategy that paid dividends on many a Saturday morning when we "fit the profile."

There are so many stories I could tell of scary moments with cops in Philadelphia and cops and strangers in the middle of nowhere; weird or disrespectful interactions in gas stations, stores, restaurants, hotel desks and lobbies; and the questioning looks and comments from White school secretaries and campus cops. They have become part of my mental and emotional fabric over time, each incident adding cumulatively to the stress of living as a Black man in America. The pain and anxiety do indeed go deeper than the skin.

Looking back, I now understand that the additional challenges and difficult situations Kim and I faced as a young Black couple created an unbelievably high level of stress for us. It was necessary for both of us to be on alert twenty-four hours a day, seven days a week, 365 days a year. Trouble could be expected to surface in any state, at any time. Kim was constantly on alert, even more than I, because of the inherent danger that Black women have had to face historically, with senseless violence aimed at them and visited on their male partners. She took on those situations with a fierceness that I later realized was matched in its intensity by a deep reservoir of fear and anger. Her fear was probably double mine, knowing that I would likely be the first target of any violence that, if perpetrated, would leave her alone to fend for herself and pick up the pieces. I became more respectful of that dilemma as the years went on.

Some interactions, after the fact, have also been amusing. One night I was returning from a recording session that had gone on too long. I'd gotten caught up in mixing tracks for the album *In the Heat of the Summer*, and the hours had simply gotten away from me. The studio was located about an hour away from the home Kim and I had moved to in Middleburgh, New York, so after bidding the engineer goodnight, I began my drive home.

Besides Albany, Schenectady, and Kingston, there are not many communities in that area of upstate New York where people of color live in any great number. It was now about 2:30 a.m., and I was thirty minutes from home when I saw those all-too-familiar flashing lights in my rearview mirror and reflecting off the trees in the darkness of an otherwise deserted country highway. I knew I had not been speeding, so I pulled my car to the side of the road and began to prepare myself for the usual exercise of civility, tension, and uncertainty.

"Hello, officer. Is there a problem?" (That's an important opening and one that African Americans learn during "the Talk" at an early age.) Having rolled down the window, I was surprised to see that the New York State trooper who had pulled me over was an African American man.

"Where are you coming from?" he asked.

"A recording session in Germantown. I'm a musician, and it's been a very long day." (Part of the Talk routine is to start to share some part of who you are or what you do to encourage the cop to hopefully begin to see you as a person.)

He cut straight to the chase. "Are you aware that you have a headlight out?"

"No sir! I had no idea. They looked fine to me."

"Can I see your license and registration?"

"Of course!" And I, well trained and practiced, had placed both on the dashboard where he could see what I was reaching for. I handed them through the window and upon taking them, he turned and began walking back to his car.

I was watching him in my side mirror (a thing I was also trained to do) and was surprised to see him stop walking before he reached his vehicle. I saw him staring at my license, and then he turned and returned to my car.

He looked at me as if registering something for the first time and then said,

"Middleburgh? You live in Middleburgh?"

"Yes, sir."

A pause and then a smile. "What the hell are you doing living in Middleburgh?"

I smiled and made a brief explanation of how we had found a house we could afford and despite it being a very conservative, rural White area we had decided to try it and had been living there for some time.

"Damn!" he snorted. "All right, my brother. Get that headlight fixed and have a good night! Good luck!"

Another amusing encounter happened after a show at a

college in Austin, Minnesota. On the way to the hotel, we stopped at a supermarket to pick up a late-night snack and some supplies for the next few days. We were approached inside the store by a very excited Black man who, after passing by the aisle where we were standing, came roaring up to us with his cart and joyfully said "Hi! Have you moved here?"

"Uh, no! We're just in town for the night. We performed over at the college earlier, and we head to another gig tomorrow."

By now his smile was gone. It turns out he was transferred there to work for Hormel and was suffering a serious bout of "I'm the only Black executive and one of few people of color in town." We talked for twenty minutes, then wished him well and were on our way.

I am grateful that those earlier days have been replaced by chain hotels, chain restaurants, and national truck stops. Those establishments, cell phones, and travel apps have made traveling as a Black person feel much safer, in a world where you can still become a George Floyd or a Trayvon Martin in a New York minute. Cell phone videos have made millions more White people aware that all those stories we tell about incidents with cops or while traveling are real.

Increasing White people's awareness of this systematic carnage, and shifting their willingness to condone it, is an important step in finding true justice. Sadly, the lives of people like Sandra Bland, Philando Castille, Terence Crutcher, and thousands of others will still be lost when this national scourge of shameful injustice is ended. I consider myself lucky, with all the miles I've traveled, to still be among those who are not on that list.

CHAPTER ELEVEN

OUT IN THE COUNTRY

In 1988, Kim and I made the major decision to move from our hometown of Philadelphia to a small town in upstate New York called Middleburgh. After living happily for many years in Mount Airy, a moderately upscale and diverse section of Philly, years of life on the road made returning home to the busy pace of city life harder and harder to take. Many things combined to make city life less appealing, from traumatic events such as the MOVE bombing in 1985 to neighbor kids blasting rock and hip-hop grooves for hours each day and the lack of a good space for writing and recording new material. (Many of my demo recordings of the time featured one particular neighborhood dog barking in the wrong key.)

It's hard to say when my first thoughts of living out in the country took root. Growing up in my crowded North Philly neighborhood of rowhouses and concrete, I felt very well adapted to city life, with its almost constant noise from cars, trolleys, buses, and trucks rumbling at all hours. The life-interrupting sounds of police and ambulance sirens competed for our attention, cascading their warnings throughout our blocks and blocks of row houses. I was used to the chaos and noise, but that doesn't mean it wasn't affecting me on many levels.

For relief, there were family outings or holiday trips to Fairmont Park (the largest city park in the nation at 9,200 acres), where we might have a barbecue, play games, or go swimming. The fauna I came across in those days were typically stray and neighbors' dogs, feral cats, pigeons and other city dwelling birds, flyover birds, and periodic encounters with raccoons, foxes, or deer. Now and then, one of the greatly feared and mythic city sewer rats would make a terrifying appearance, darting across a street on its way from one underground opening to another, to the dismay of anyone so unfortunate to be on the scene.

The flora of my world were mostly contained in small flower beds kept by persistent and resourceful green-thumbed neighbors managing postage stamp-sized grass lawns that added more color than cover to the stark surroundings. There was only one tree on my block. It was not a great representative of its species, nor did it provide any appreciable shade on those blazing hot summer afternoons. In those years, before environmental awareness was in the public consciousness, we didn't realize the benefits that trees and green spaces bring in reducing stress and improving the quality of life—not to mention their cooling effect on the pavement in hot summer weather. On the other hand, our parents and neighbors were glad to have no leaves to rake up in the fall.

But throughout my childhood, I was blessed to have a few connections that gave me a taste of the difference between my city existence and the quieter, more tranquil beauty of the country life I saw on TV or in movies. For years, my church operated a camp and conference center on land they owned thirty miles north of Philadelphia in Lahaska, Pennsylvania, near Doylestown. That property, rumored to have been a stop on the Underground Railroad in the 1800s, gave us church kids and our adults a perfect place to have a country getaway in the summer months.

There were also infrequent but memorable trips to the South to visit relatives in Richmond, Culpepper, and other rural Virginia spots. Those brief trips were often marred by experiences of segregation and tempered by the necessary caution of relatives who worried and worked to make sure there would be no Emmett Tills in our family. But being in the South also increased my experiences of dark, quiet nights, wild animals, and the ways of living among country folk. There was a slowness to the days and a peacefulness to the nights that we didn't experience in Philly. By the time I heard and fell in love with the song "Out in the Country" (sung by my favorite rock band during high school, Three Dog Night), I had begun telling my friends that I planned to live in a cabin out in the woods, with a really cool dog, when I got older. The thought felt magical and gave my cluttered world some sense of purpose and space.

> Whenever I need to leave it all behind
> Or feel the need to get away
> I find a quiet place, far from the human race
> Out in the country.
>
> Before the breathin' air is gone
> Before the sun is just a bright spot in the night-time
> Out where the rivers like to run
> I stand alone and take back somethin' worth rememberin'.
> —"Out in the Country" by Paul H. Williams
> and Roger S. Nichols

As fate would have it, around the time Kim and I decided to look for a more hospitable living environment outside of our hometown, we met Sonny Ochs, the older sister of the famous political singer/songwriter Phil Ochs. As we became good friends, she not only invited us to perform at a number of Phil Ochs Song Nights across the nation but also hosted us in a delightful concert series she ran near her home outside Middleburgh.

Sonny's house in the middle of the woods was so tranquil and quiet that staying with her was quite rejuvenating. Her neighbors—many of them transplants from New York City and other locales—were thoughtful and interesting, leading us to feel like it would be a good community to be a part of. She happened to be selling real estate in the area of Middleburgh at that time to supplement her income, and she encouraged us to buy a couple of acres of land as an investment and a place to build the cabin in the woods I'd dreamed about. Sonny was hoping to create a musician/artist colony in the area, and fellow musicians Terry Leonino and Greg Artzner (the musical duo Magpie—who would later become our friends and collaborators), musician/comedian Nancy Tucker, and others had also recently bought land nearby. Even though it brought back images of my earlier thoughts of a home in the country, when faced with the reality, the prospect of buying land in a rural wilderness (it felt like the middle of freakin' nowhere to me!) suddenly felt like quite a stretch. Nonetheless, Kim and I went on a land-shopping trip with Sonny and unexpectedly found the house where I have resided for the last thirty-four years. Seeing a picture of that house on the wall of Sonny's real estate office led us to make a visit that turned into "We have to live here!"

Our decision to relocate prompted a furious and challenging move and a transition from being city residents to country residents, a shift that required summoning our courage. We quickly realized that moving five hours and a universe away from what we knew (a city where both of us were born, with great cultural and ethnic diversity and access to support from our families) to a country town in an area that was mostly White, very conservative, and filled with many unknowns would be no small thing. We hoped, without real evidence, that we were up to the adventure.

The town of Middleburgh was settled in 1712 and is located in Schoharie County, New York. The area is often called the breadbasket of the Revolution, denoting its history as a fertile farming community for hundreds of years. We knew next to nothing about the area or about how the community would accept a Black couple moving in to live as neighbors. (We did hear one story from a relative of the folks who sold us the house that they "had thoughts" about not selling to Black people. The relative countered, "It's been on the market for months. You wanna sell your house or not?") They quickly agreed to make the sale.

But we believed from our interactions on several visits to the area that we had met enough like-minded people who cared enough to come to our aid if and when an incident arose. The fact that we were also something of a "celebrity couple" (we had already done some events for community benefit before we moved) helped put us in a bit of a special category that "ordinary" Black folks moving in would not necessarily enjoy. This would later prove to be helpful in a number of ways.

After a departure in Philly that was filled with goodbyes,

tears (from Kim's sister, mostly), and more private thoughts of "are we sure we wanna do this?" we were greeted by a bevy of new neighbors and area folks that Sonny had gathered to help us get into the house. It was a joyful welcome and started the adventure off just right. The mover, a Black man from Philly with a truck and two sons, was impressed by this amazing group of helpers that made his work so much easier. But he did pull me aside as I paid him to say, "I wish you well, but keep my number—just in case?" I assured him, laughingly, "We'll be fine!" I hoped I was right.

I am happy to say that over these thirty-four years in Middleburgh, there has been no major incident or glaring racial indignity to deal with or recover from. There have been many small to medium moments of awkwardness, ranging from bemused or unsavory looks in local stores to area kerfuffles around race (a local mayor and county supervisor were taped making ugly, racist comments after President Obama was elected), with a few moments of deep concern mixed in. I've endured a few utterances of the N-word. But there have also been lots of enjoyable concerts, dinners, educational visits to the local schools, and celebrations.

I was assistant coach for the girls' varsity basketball team at the local high school for fourteen years and helped run a basketball camp for five years before that. Some of the parents of those girls showed signs of being uncomfortable when they came face to face with me during or after practice or games, but everyone survived relatively intact, and by season's end there were mostly smiles and thanks. I still hear from or run into some of the young women I coached, who tell me that I was the first person of color with whom they had multiple conversations or a personal relationship. Many of my former players have gone on to become teachers or professionals who work on racial equity or diversity issues in their jobs, schools, or families. One surprised me not long ago with news that she now leads civil rights journeys to the South for students and staff at her school near Albany. I see on Facebook or Instagram that some are in mixed-race relationships. Others who came to me when they found themselves dealing with overwhelming pressures of being "the other" in a sea of White cultural complexity and social abuse are now clearly moving through life on solid ground. Most of them never mention the subject of race or recall long past moments of tension as we reconnect, but I like to think that perhaps our interactions provided some widening of perspective beyond the limitations of this close, conservative, homogenous community.

In the 1990s, I served as a member of a local task force that was formed to deal with a complaint that our local school district was negligent in providing a safe physical and emotional environment for the lone Black male student at the high school at that time. He was getting beaten up every day by White students. When confronted with the situation, school officials advised the family that "he would just have to toughen up." The family took their case to the Equal Opportunities Commission who, after an investigation, directed the district to resolve the situation equitably and to design and implement a nondiscrimination policy. It was a tense time. After many meetings and some required training, the issue was resolved. But, as with racial issues across the nation, that resolution continues to require attention and monitoring.

As you might imagine, some of the new experiences Kim

and I encountered in "the Burg," as the locals call it, were more of the variety of city folks moving to the country and having to learn new things. Some were amusing and some were not, like the care and feeding of a septic system and what it feels like to dig one out by hand. I found out from the previous owner (who was now my auto mechanic) that the septic tank was located in an area that could not be accessed by machine. That experience took the better part of two months during brutally hot days. At the end, I was saved by two local boy scouts who dug the last part with me, standing in a septic archive zone (yes, another term for excrement) exclaiming, "This is better than Pioneer training!"

I learned the value of knowing a great plumber who makes late night or early morning house calls and teaches you things from project to project. We also learned how to be patient with people who may take a full eight or ten years to stop asking "So, are you up for the weekend?" Being a transplant to a rural area can be trying and requires patience and skill at being on the lean end of trust.

I have been the first Black person that White people have interacted with so often that it has become an integral part of who I am. I have learned much from being in those situations and use that knowledge every day. I've learned to use my observational skills and my ability to ask questions to reveal underlying prejudice and racism that others might miss. I've learned not to jump right into information-sharing mode and to look for phrases that create connection. I've learned that change comes from establishing a relationship and that balance and openness leave room for the possibility of relationships developing. It can take years.

I learned that a visit to a local store is not always just about getting what you need. It's a time of community exchange and news gathering. The lesson is, be friendly and don't be in a hurry. When the clerk says, "So, how's things?" if you linger a bit, you may find out some useful information or deepen the connection. And then when you really need something in haste, they're likely to be more ready and willing to come through and fit you in with joy. I also learned that it's often a valuable investment to listen to the personal stories that seem unrelated to what you asked. Context and perspective don't always run in a straight line. And living your values is much better than mouthing them.

In Philadelphia, we'd feed the old bread scraps to the birds and they would gobble it down. I soon found out that country birds won't touch the stuff. We'd throw bread out to the birds in Middleburgh, and days later it was still lying on the patio. The birds were totally dismissive. "Damn city people! What do they think we are, pigeons? Get some birdseed, dude."

When we did put up a proper bird feeder, feeding the birds provided a different kind of close, personal encounter with nature as well. One day, returning from a tour, we noticed that there was a rather large pawprint, four feet up, in the middle our double glass door where a feeder had been. Days later, coming up the driveway from a grocery run, I noticed movement off the patio. I stopped and watched as a bobcat sauntered off the patio. It locked eyes with me, then slowly turned and loped up into the woods without ever breaking stride. That feeder was never replaced.

I learned that you best not talk negatively about *anybody* to *anybody*, even when you think you know them very well.

Names might be different, but lots of folks will be related to each other. I learned to listen more than I talk.

I learned to be gracious when neighbors drop by unannounced to say hi and chat. Often they'll give good advice on something they noticed, and it might be something helpful for you to know, such as, "Did you see those bear tracks down your driveway? You might want to be a bit careful going out to the car at night." Me: "A bear?! Where? What tracks?!"

I learned that when the person who sold you the house three years earlier roars up late one night with six others on snowmobiles and asks (after your heart stops beating in fear and shock) if you want to go for your first snowmobile ride through the woods on trails you didn't know existed, say, "Yes!" It was breathtaking. That's how progress, better relations, and friendships are made.

Perhaps the experience that most exemplifies living in the country was when the bridge that leads from the road to our shared driveway was washed out by Hurricane Irene. I found myself wading through (and a few times in) Brooky Creek every day for eight months to get to and from my car until the bridge was repaired. The county let us know that they would not be replacing the bridge because it was on our property and it was not their responsibility. With FEMA granting us a very modest settlement, we faced the overwhelming task of raising the additional $20,000 that would enable us to hire a local contractor to rebuild the bridge.

That challenge gave us another lesson in the power of song. Our local and regional neighbors held a series of fundraising concerts at which we performed. And when news of our predicament spread to people in our global music community—from as far away as Austria and Australia—folks responded generously with donations that allowed us to get the bridge rebuilt. Its repair is a testament to the belief that when you work to help others with compassion and an open heart, it often will come back to you when you find yourself in need.

I mentioned earlier that Middleburgh, like much of upstate New York, is politically very conservative. In current-day parlance, our county is significantly more red than blue. In 1989, that was even more true. On my first opportunity to vote in an election in Middleburgh I made sure that I was registered, and on primary day I drove up to my polling place at the firehouse two miles from my house. There were no cars in the parking lot, no line, and no visible evidence of humans anywhere. But I entered the fire station, ambled past the two fire trucks, and walked into an auxiliary room where two women sat at a table.

"Good afternoon, young man. So nice to have you," said one of the women. "You've come to vote?"

"Yes, ma'am, I certainly have."

"Well, you've come to the right place," said woman number two. "What's your name?" "Reggie Harris. I moved in a while ago and live just down the road."

The first woman said, "Yes, I think you're living in the old Mickle place. Is that right?" (Small town indeed!)

"Actually, I'm living in the house across the driveway, and yes, this is my first time voting here in town."

The second woman began to scan her voting list and was still scanning when she looked up and said, "I'm not seeing your name here. Are you a Republican or an Independent?"

I paused and then said, "I'm a Democrat." Both women looked at each other, and then with a puzzled look on her face, the first woman said, "Oh! You know they don't have a primary, right?"

I didn't know. Apparently, there were so few Democrats in town that the Democratic party didn't even bother to hold a primary for their candidate!

But things have changed in my three decades of living in the area. A few years after my encounter with the voting ladies, a Senate candidate named Hillary Clinton came to the area and held two Town Hall meetings, impressing enough people that a Democratic primary was established. She won, and things began to change for the better.

And now a group of citizens has formed an organization called Rural Awakenings that works hard to promote bipartisan and common-sense political activism. We have now established a positive presence for progressive change, better race relations, and reform. In 2016, our region elected its first African American congressmember, Antonio Delgado. He's doing a great job representing all the people and was re-elected in 2018 and 2020. He is now Lieutenant Governor of New York State, having been appointed by Governor Kathy Hochul in May 2022.

In another sign of positive change, a local committee was formed and charged with reviewing police policies and protocols, answering the call of a statewide mandate from the governor on the heels of the protests and videos following the deaths of George Floyd, Elijah McClain, and Breonna Taylor. The committee, of which I am a member, is charged to consider new language and policies that might help to avoid the rampant police killings and abuse of people of color that have been the norm around the nation for much too long.

I shared with this committee—which includes the mayor of Cobleskill, the chief of police, the district attorney, and other area residents—the stories that I related in earlier chapters about being frequently stopped by police and state troopers. Whenever someone says, "Well, we don't have that problem here!" I've shared my experiences of difficult and traumatic interactions with the police. Before cell phone videos began showing the truth of this American problem, it was easy for White people to think it wasn't real. While the frequency and severity of violent or unpleasant encounters between police and people of color in Schoharie County are not at the same level as in large cities, I share my stories to show that implicit bias, racial prejudice, and hateful attitudes are very much alive and at issue in our area. Fortunately, everyone in the room seemed to understand. Hopefully that understanding will lead to making a difference.

I've found great friendships and opportunities for learning out in the country. Since deciding to make it my home, I have also tried to impart goodwill and useful knowledge. The cultural climate hasn't always been easy, but I have great memories of our community coming together to celebrate, recover from loss, worship, party, and play with joy and abandon. There have also been solemn moments of shared pain and sorrow, such as the burying of residents and loved ones, and living through the devastation of Hurricane Irene that almost wiped our community off the map and left so many of us having to dig out, rebuild, and start again.

Life in Middleburgh has been a complex mix of unique friendship circles, individual freedom, and personal, regional, and global misunderstandings. On any given day, life here requires cool, wise heads to find a way to connect and do what must be done. Most often, it is done without selfishness or bias and with a healthy serving of community care and concern. It's been a place where I have found enough refuge from a loud and conflicted world to write, rest, breathe, and recharge my spirit so I can go out once again to love and serve the world.

> Whenever I feel them closing in on me
> Or need a bit of room to move
> When life becomes too fast, I find relief at last
> Out in the country

CHAPTER TWELVE

I HAVE NO PEOPLE . . . OR DO I?

One of my favorite books is *Native Stranger: A Black American's Journey into the Heart of Africa*. The author, Eddy L. Harris, wrote four books that I read in succession, starting with *Mississippi Solo* in 1989. Mr. Harris (no relation) is an African American writer whose books chronicle his travels around the United States and throughout the African continent on journeys that explored his sense of place and his relationship to history. I was introduced to his writing by a friend who said she thought I would enjoy *Mississippi Solo* as an entertaining memoir of his ill-advised, near-fatal adventures while canoeing the entire Mississippi River, from its headwaters in Minnesota to its end in the Gulf of Mexico. He did this all by his lonesome, as the title implies.

I was hooked right from the start. His journey began with some impulsive and clueless arrogance regarding what he needed to know and pack for the voyage. Reading with unabashed excitement and some jealousy, I appreciated his willing spirit. Kim and I had launched ourselves out on tours around the nation with that same joie de vivre and had endured some arduous experiences of our own, such as driving for hours through winter storms to reach concert venues, or driving from

Philly to Tennessee, South Dakota, New York, and back in seven days to pick up gigs. We needed the money.

Eddy's adventures were dangerous and troublesome, as he was camping, canoeing, and living out in the elements. He was often hampered by poor planning, and his dangerous near misses and hardships reminded me of all the times on the road when we unknowingly placed ourselves in tight situations (or knew full well but did it anyway). We had learned, for example, that being a minority in Iowa or South Dakota was a very different thing than it was in New York or New Jersey. We learned to keep a low profile on the road. Still, we were often the recipients of grace, charity, and a whole lot of luck.

I remember one midwinter tour of Minnesota during which Kim and I found ourselves driving after a snowstorm, along with our keyboard player Conrad Krider. We were on a highway that had been cleared for travel but had snowbanks piled up just off the road. We were trying to get to Carleton College, a small, liberal arts college in Northfield, Minnesota, for a concert. Using a road atlas, we realized that we had made an errant turn and were going in the wrong direction. (The joys of GPS were well off in the future.) We decided to make a U-turn on this two-lane road and acted without thinking clearly about the road conditions. As it happened, the plow had cleared the snow only to the edges, leaving the areas just off the road untouched. On making our turn, the van sunk into the fresh snow on the shoulder and we were instantly stuck. Several panicked moments went by as we stood on this lonely road, Easterners and neophyte roadsters wondering what to do.

As we stood getting colder by the minute, as if by miracle, two pickup trucks approached us, one coming from each direction. We were wondering if we should try to flag them down when they, each on their own, slowed and stopped. The entire following exchange took less than a minute.

"You stuck?" called the driver headed in our direction.

"Yes, sir, we are!"

The driver going the other way rolled down his window and chimed in "Which way you headed?"

"Back that way!" I pointed in reply.

Without another word to each other or to us, they each were out of their vehicles and at the back and side of our van in seconds.

"Turn your wheel to the left and gun it when I say go!" the second driver said. And with four of us pushing and Kim behind the wheel, our van lurched forward, lifted out of the snowbank, back onto the road and around to the other side. I turned to say thanks, only to realize that they were both closing their vehicle doors and, mission accomplished, waved and were off to their destinations. We appreciated the Midwestern kindness!

Just like Eddy, we learned a lot of valuable lessons on our journeys, traveling over 70,000 miles by car each year to perform at colleges, schools, churches, and coffeehouses across America. As another African American man traveling the country at the same time as Eddy—albeit in a duo—I was captivated and informed by his writing. His fearless spirit seemed to help him cast off the anxieties that might limit him from experiencing life and fully exploring the vistas of his imagination.

His next memoir, *Native Stranger: A Black American's Journey into the Heart of Africa*, told of a year-long excursion on the continent of Africa that he took with no prescribed plan for where his journeys might take him. It turned out to be another fascinating read, as his adventures once again proved fun, perilous, and unnerving. Most of all, his discoveries about his disconnect with the "African homeland" proved enlightening. In the first paragraph he writes: "Because my skin is black you will say that I traveled Africa to find the roots of my race. I did not—unless that race is the human race, for except for the color of my skin, I am not African. If I didn't know it then, I know it now."

His statement "I am not African" is one that I've heard uttered many times by other Black travelers who visit the continent of our ancestors. They found that being hundreds of years removed from a physical connection with Africa imparts a cloudiness to our relationship to the place and can impair our ability to fully and confidently claim our racial identity.

My ancestors were stolen from Africa over 350 years ago and by all accounts came to the United States by way of the West Indies before landing in Virginia. As a result of that roundabout journey and the various ways we have been genetically and socially tossed and turned, the identities of most African Americans are constantly under repair and redefinition. The African American sociologist (and first Black man to receive a PhD from Harvard University) W.E.B. Dubois established the concept of "double consciousness" in his groundbreaking book *The Souls of Black Folk*. In that work he reveals how oppression, the effects of slavery, and the ongoing presence of racism have made most African Americans feel that their identity is divided into several parts, making it difficult or impossible to have one unified identity. We are made to see ourselves through the lens of others—White people, White institutions, media portrayals—and that process produces intergenerational stress, tension, self-contempt, and recriminations from inside and outside the African American community.

These factors contribute to the fact that Black people suffer more anxiety, contract more illnesses, and statistically die at a younger age than White people, despite our storied, spontaneously joyful cultural presence and the resilience reflected in our language and our music. Research shows that the messages we receive from a variety of societal sources cause us to develop negative feelings about ourselves and about each other, known as internalized oppression. It's a hard game to win or overcome, especially in a culture where most White people think we're all playing on a level field.

As a young adult, struggling with my racial identity and in an effort to rid myself of that stressful pressure, I took the position that "I have no people!" and declared myself a "free agent human being." If that's not an example of a young mind doing mental gymnastics to hurtle a critical obstacle, I don't know what is!

As I've mentioned in other parts of this book, my early cultural grounding has been a great benefit to me as a person and as an artist. But it has taken many years of mentoring, counseling, and some very focused personal and emotional homework to connect me to the healthier aspects of being a Black artist, musician, and citizen in America. I am forever grateful that being an "artiste" gave me license to exercise some freedom of thought and expression that many young people of my background do not enjoy, and that my alternative life path as a musician and my interactions with supportive allies in the White world connected me to places, people, and experiences that helped me thrive as a human being.

In addition, personal research and study have been particularly helpful in connecting me to the true history and accomplishments of people who had already walked many miles down the road of being Black in America. I studied musician activists like Louis Armstrong, Matt Jones, Odetta, Josh White Jr., Bernice Johnson Reagon, and Richie Havens, as well as other famous African Americans like Jackie Robinson, Frederick Douglass, Madame C.J. Walker, Matthew A. Henson, Diahann Carroll, Sidney Poitier, and Malcolm X—people whose lives I could observe and try to emulate. I absorbed how Black folks found refuge, inspiration, pride, and stability in the songs, stories, and rhythms that we now know as the bedrock of the African American experience. It reinforced the critical importance of young people of color being able to see and connect with successful people who look like them.

For me, one of those people was Harry Belafonte. As a child, I loved hearing him sing "Scarlet Ribbons" or "The Banana Boat Song" as it came through my mom's radio as she got ready for work in the darkness of a weekday winter morning. I would lie on Mom's bed and let that voice wash over me. Watching him on the *Ed Sullivan Show* and other programs, I was impressed by this handsome, dignified, and articulate man who modeled being a strong Black figure of self-pride and determination. He was an outspoken voice for civil rights, a standard bearer for our race, and he made our people proud. It was a special pleasure for me to meet him in person, which happened twice.

My first encounter with him came in fall 1994 at 6:00 a.m. one morning in a nearly empty Cincinnati airport. We had both come to town to perform (at different times and locations) for the opening of the National Underground Railroad Freedom Center. Walking toward each other, each on our way to catch planes to other gigs, I recognized him right away and decided to seize the moment. I put myself in his path and stopped a few feet before him blocking his way. "Good morning!" I offered. He smiled a weary smile, paused, and returned the greeting. We chatted briefly, and then I stepped out of his way so we could catch our flights. In 2014 we met again, as participants in the Pete Seeger tribute concert at Lincoln Center in New York City. That day we had a longer conversation, and I thanked him for being a role model for me and so many others. He was gracious on both occasions. Until the day he died, he remained an unapologetic voice for social change.

Another role model of strength and persistence in my early years was Rosa Parks, who sat down to stand up. She held the attention of our community nationwide as a fearless resistor of oppression whose actions demanded dignity. Kim and I had the privilege to meet her in 1989 when we were invited to perform at the 25th anniversary gathering of the 1964 Mississippi Freedom Summer Project at Queens College in New York. For thirty minutes we shared a green room with that icon of courage and then had the honor of introducing her in story and song. It intrigues me that such a quiet, semi-demure woman was the center of such a powerful protest. She's a woman of few words, but just being in her presence for those moments infused me with a strength that I carry with me to this day.

As I continued my personal studies in African American history, the work of Carter G. Woodson—the noted scholar and historian of African American life—helped me appreciate the legacy of my people which, at that time, was a hidden history in America. I began to be aware of the resilience of the African American community while learning the stories of Harriet Tubman, Richard Allen, George Washington Carver, and W.E.B. DuBois.

In searching for a workable framework as Kim and I forged our way as a Black folk music duo, we faced the constant question, "How do you describe yourselves, anyway?" We came to realize that there was no accurate description for what we were doing. Our folk/pop inspired mix of songs, arranged in the context of our classical and gospel flavored roots, were often said to be "too Black" for many White audiences, "too White" for Black audiences, and "too pop" for folk audiences. We were a musical hybrid, neither fish nor fowl. Our saving grace was this: Whatever it was we were doing, we were attractive and skillful, and we sounded good.

Having lived in that racial/cultural limbo since junior high school, the effects really began to wear on me when we were twenty years into our music career. Success was limited by the constantly annoying specter of race, and we both were still having lots of trouble with self-acceptance. This was the case despite the fact that we had found a credible way to express our ethnic heritage and our creative artistic energies with programs on the Underground Railroad and the music of the modern civil rights movement. Almost all musicians have hard stories about paying their dues. But just as African American citizens had to pay a poll tax or jump through other hoops to vote, get work, or get access to the mainstream world, we felt ourselves subject to having to pay a skin tax in order to be seen, heard, and considered as worthy as White people of gaining access to a clearly segregated music world.

After years of struggling through that gauntlet, we were both experts at denying that the stress was taking its toll. The results surfaced in several illnesses, including one that would eventually require a liver transplant for me. And then, at just the right time, came an event that proved to be the start of the powerful healing that I'd needed for a long time. It came in an unexpected remedy so profound that it still reverberates in my body and spirit to this day. That remedy came on October 16, 1995: the Million Man March.

The march was the brainchild of Minister Louis Farrakhan of the Nation of Islam, formerly also known in the community as the Black Muslims. Mr. Farrakhan announced the idea in June of that year: an event focused on Black community unity and aimed at combating perceived negative racial stereotypes in media and popular culture. Farrakhan offered to collaborate with other Black organizations and leaders in his call for one million men of color to come to the nation's capital for a day of reflection and renewal. The Nation of Islam had long been controversial inside and outside of the Black community for being aggressively dismissive or hostile to White people, Jews, and any non-Muslim Black people who worked with them. This was a problem.

Given the political, racial, and religious ramifications of Mr. Farrakhan's past and present attitudes, a vigorous debate arose around the nation as to whether this idea, hatched by such a polarizing figure, could ever gain credibility. It divided Black and White allies, and even inside the Black community many were not supportive.

I followed the debate from a distance and initially decided that I would not attend. With my personal and professional focus on cross-cultural dialogue and bridge building, I didn't see how this would help in my work. But before long, the date and details were set, speakers were scheduled, and it became evident that the march was building momentum and was going to happen. But I could not decide if this gathering was right for me.

About a week before the event, I was still considering. Then on Sunday, October 8, I opened the Sunday *New York Times* to find a full-page ad sponsored by the Jewish service organization B'nai Brith, demanding that African American men of good conscience not attend the march. I have to admit that seeing a full-page ad in the one of the nation's leading newspapers addressed to men like me was a shock. In addition to the unexpectedness of seeing an ad in the *New York Times* addressed to Black men, the substance of the ad triggered a deep visceral response that took me by surprise.

I was sympathetic to the fact that many in the Jewish community were voicing concern and dismay about the fact this event was sponsored by Louis Farrakhan, who had directed much of his most hateful rhetoric and ire toward Jews. They were not the only ones voicing this view. Opposition to Farrakhan's presence and prominent participation in the planning came from many quarters, including significant leaders of the Black community.

But having spent almost twenty years researching and presenting African American history, with its consistent theme of the constant indignity of having individual and community actions, integrity, and deliberations subjugated to the scrutiny and control of others, I felt intensely that the ad was an intrusion into our intra-community dialogue.

I understood the perspective of the larger Jewish community, which for decades had been a key ally for the Black community in the modern civil rights movement. I was also acutely aware that existing tensions between Black and Jewish people had produced rifts in that long-standing relationship, such as the holdover frictions from the days when Black Power advocates expelled White people (many of them Jews) from that very movement. And there was current-day anger in the Black community generated by the ongoing conflicts between Israel and the Palestinians. All of this was in the mix. But to me, the wording of the ad, centered on who had the right to a voice in Black dialogue in the US, felt like inappropriate interference into the affairs of the Black community. It made me angry enough to reconsider going to the march to add my voice, despite my own misgivings.

I decided to call my friend Rabbi Jonathan Kligler to do what we did frequently—chat and turn things over. He listened, I listened. He talked, and I talked. We agreed and disagreed. It was a tough, emotional, and ultimately satisfying discussion. At the end, he said, "Follow your heart, and let me know what you decide."

I followed that call with one to my friend Dr. Ade Knowles, a noted musician who had been a member of Gil Scott Heron and the Midnight Band and who was at that time the Vice President for Student Affairs at Rensselaer Polytechnic Institute in Troy, New York. We talked at length—as friends and brothers—about the march, weighing the pros and cons of attending. I told him that I had finally come to the decision that I did indeed have a people, and after a spirited discussion we made plans to go to the march together.

Early on the morning of October 16, Ade and I met over breakfast with two of his longtime friends, a physician from New Jersey and a Wall Street broker from New York, at a hotel near Union Station in D.C. Our conversation started slowly, but soon became energized. Hardly able to contain our excitement, each of us was eager to list our reasons for coming to the event. I shared that even though I had taken two trains on the Metro I had encountered almost no White people on my entire journey into the city that day. Two of the few White faces I saw, a male/female couple, had approached me as I stood intently looking at the Metro train map, trying to decide which train I needed for my transfer.

"Are you headed to the March?" they asked excitedly.

"Yes, I am."

"Do you need help? You know which train to take?" I couldn't help but smile at their awkward but clearly well-intentioned excitement.

"Yes, I'm just checking, but I'm good," I said with a smile.

With that they both called out, "Have a good day," as they hustled off.

I recounted that story to my new companions, and we shared some reservations about possible safety issues. But these concerns were overcome by our shared feelings of purpose, excitement, and joyful anticipation. This was going to be somethin' else, of that we were sure.

We made our way to find a place on the national mall, with hundreds of thousands of men—and some women—from all directions, to see what this day would bring. I could spend the rest of this book trying to unpack the impact of the conversations, the speeches, the music, the arguments, the

sighs of agreement, the tears, and the healing that happened
for me that day, and it would still not do it justice. Black men
from every corner of the world put their lives aside that day to
join hundreds of thousands of their fellows. The day included
speeches, music, and reflections from a diverse group of speakers, including Washington, D.C., mayor Marion Barry; civil
rights legends Rev. Joseph Lowery, Rosa Parks, and Dorothy
Height; poet Maya Angelou; Dr. Cornell West; Stevie Wonder; and yes, Minister Louis Farrakhan, all contributing something useful to the day.

How many people were there? The actual number remains
in question depending on the reporting source. It doesn't matter to me. The miraculous power of that day was that it was
one of the first days of my life where I felt free to look around
at my surroundings, look at the color of my hands, take a deep
breath, and not feel a need to explain or be ashamed of who
I was. I didn't need to worry about who I might become or
wonder who was fearful of me. I saw in those other faces a
hope that was evident in the words of one of the songs we sang
near the start of the day, a song now known as the African
American national anthem, "Lift Every Voice and Sing."

> Lift ev'ry voice and sing 'til earth and heaven ring
> Ring with the harmonies of Liberty
> Let our rejoicing rise, high as the list'ning skies
> Let it resound loud as the rolling sea
> Sing a song full of the faith that the dark past has taught us
> Sing a song full of the hope that the present has brought us
> Facing the rising sun of our new day begun
> Let us march on 'til victory is won

I left the march that night in the middle of Mr. Farrakhan's speech and said goodbye to Ade and my new brothers. I got back on the Metro and returned to where I was staying, thinking new thoughts of freedom and possibility. The next morning, testing my newfound emotional wellness, I walked into a music store in Takoma Park, Maryland. I was looking to buy some new strings for my guitar. I walked into a situation where, a day earlier, I would have activated my "Hi! I'm a friendly Black person! Don't be alarmed by my presence" persona, to put the startled White clerks—who looked at me with that look that I've seen thousands of times—at ease. It's a fearful look that says, "Who is this Black stranger entering our store?" But on this new day, with a new sense of who I was and what my mission was, I simply said, "Morning!" And then without another word, I walked with dignity to the guitar section and without looking back, embraced my new attitude with self-assured purpose and freedom.

CHAPTER THIRTEEN

A SECOND CHANCE AT LIFE

In my days as a student at Temple University, I had become a regular blood donor. I would like to attribute this desire to help those in need to my then-burgeoning attitude toward community responsibility. But in retrospect, I'm convinced that I was also lured into making those frequent contributions by the generous offering of powdered doughnuts that were available at the end of the procedure in an all-you-can-eat buffet of doughnuts, pretzels, and juice. Snack heaven! Those little white powdered doughnuts are not really my favorites—I prefer crème-filled or chocolate iced. Nonetheless, as a perpetually hungry college student I became a regular patron of the Red Cross Blood Mobile whenever it appeared on campus looking to take advantage of the 30,000 college students roaming the row of food trucks on Broad Street. It was only a matter of time before I earned my Gallon Pin and became a full-fledged Red Cross blood donation devotee. There was no way of knowing in those years of youthful, carefree living that the act of giving blood for others would turn out to be life-changing for me some twenty years down the road.

My fateful blood donation incident happened in 1995. Kim and I were doing a performance tour of colleges in the Midwest when, during our weekly phone check-in with Kim's mom, she delivered the crushing news that one of Kim's aunts had been diagnosed with leukemia. She added that her aunt's doctors were having difficulty finding donors of blood plasma that she desperately needed. Knowing that that we were regular blood donors, Kim's mom asked if we would be willing to donate to the cause on our next trip to Philly.

Our tour lasted another two weeks, but we made an appointment at a blood donation center near our old home in the Mt. Airy section of Philadelphia and soon made the trip to the city. We were greeted with open arms (literally) and paid off in good feelings and, yes, doughnuts. (Thinking back, I often wonder why the Red Cross in Philly never thought to make a deal with the Tasty Baking Company, makers of Tastykake, another treasured Philadelphia institution, to reward donors. They would probably have had people lined up out the door.) The session went well, and I went home feeling good about my contribution to Kim's aunt's treatment needs.

Returning home, I thought little of that donation until a few weeks later when I received a letter from the Red Cross. Knowing that receiving a letter was not a normal consequence of the process, I read it with great interest. The letter began:

> Dear Mr. Harris,
>
> Thanks so much for your contribution of blood plasma. We are sorry to inform you that your blood could not be used because your liver enzyme levels were too high. We recommend that before giving again, you consult with your physician to determine what the problem might be.

I was shocked and more than a little concerned. Physically, I felt great and thought I was the picture of health in every way. I read the letter over and over, trying to imagine what might have gone wrong. After much thought, I took their suggestion to consult with my doctor, who was also a good friend back in Philadelphia. He ordered some additional tests, and we laughed that most likely it was something simple that would be easily resolved.

Imagine my surprise when the results came back and confirmed that the levels were still high and indicated no reason why. This testing was repeated several times in the next few months, and after a number of other tests ordered by a local gastroenterology specialist, we still had no answers.

Over the next year and a half, I became one of those cases that doctors take to their conferences to ask other docs what they think the issue might be. Two years after the first suspicious blood test, on Christmas Eve 1997, we got an answer. On a hunch, my new gastroenterologist, Dr. David Cohen in Schenectady, had asked me to agree to a simultaneous endoscopy and colonoscopy. I awoke from the procedure to see Kim and my friends Margie and Ed standing near my bed with grim faces. They were soon joined by Dr. Cohen, who gave me the sobering diagnosis. He explained that I had an autoimmune disease called primary sclerosing cholangitis. It is a disease of the bile ducts, in which inflammation causes scars within the bile ducts that eventually destroy the liver. I was told it is a rare disease for which there is no cure. Primary sclerosing cholangitis occurs in about one out of 100,000 people, mostly young and middle-aged men. Treatment can slow down the progression of the disease, but ultimately the patient either receives a new liver or dies. With each sentence he spoke the bad news settled into my brain and heart. Christmas joy was a goner.

On Dr. Cohen's recommendation, I set up an appointment with the Hospital of the University of Pennsylvania in Philadelphia, which had one of the best transplant units in the nation. During a long, draining, and traumatizing day, the doctors and support personnel on my new transplant team explained every aspect of the organ transplant process, from preparation steps to after care. Although it was unclear when my condition would necessitate a liver transplant, they described it as inevitable. The prospect seemed surreal, since I still had no symptoms. Despite all of their upbeat "You're in great hands!" optimism, I was devastated.

Within a year of that meeting things would begin to get worse, although I still had no idea of just how bad worse would be. Over time, I would experience a steady decline in health that produced frequent pain, fatigue, unbearable and relentless body itching, rashes, weight loss, bleeding sores, the discoloration of my eyes, skin, and hair, along with years of sleepless nights and long hard days. Because my liver could no longer remove toxins from my body, the toxins rose to the surface and exited through my skin. This was the source of my constant itchiness and resulted in needing to wash off—in a bath, a shower, or whatever I could find—several times a day. This went on for twelve years.

As the disease progressed, I faced worried looks from friends, acquaintances, my audiences, and even strangers I passed on the street, all a reminder to me that I was a sorry sight to see. People would ask, "What's wrong with you?" Not

wanting to explain my situation to everyone I met, I sometimes left the question unanswered. Many didn't ask, but their
eyes told me they were imagining the worst. On top of that,
many of the doctors I saw throughout those years, after hearing that I was a musician, would ask in a hushed voice, "Mr.
Harris, is there something you want to share about your life-
style?" (Expecting me to come clean about being a substance
abuser.) No such revelation was applicable in my case, and it
seems that despite a lifetime of clean living, I just got unlucky.

Sick or not, I had to keep working. Since we weren't artists
with a catalogue of hit songs that produced royalty checks in
the mail, the bulk of our earnings came from being in concert
somewhere. With mounting medical bills, we had to work,
and work we did. My daily regimen was to get up early after
a largely sleepless night, take a quick bath to detox and relieve
the itching, eat breakfast, maybe take another quick shower,
and then get into the car to drive to a gig, where we would
load in and set up. Then I would need to wash off, often in a
bathroom in full view of school personnel or the public, before
getting dressed to do the show. Then, at concert's end, we'd
break down, load out, and try to get to a place where I could
shower again (or maybe just rinse off, which would give more
limited relief), eat, and then do another show that afternoon or
evening. It was mind over matter most days, but not without
constant distraction and discomfort.

Days ended with the same exhausting routine: food, evening calls, a bath, and then hopefully sleep—never more than
four to five hours a night—for years. The nonstop itching was
the worst aspect of every day.

It was exhausting for me and also for Kim, who was on

call and totally involved all day, every day, to help facilitate the routine and keep the music train moving. There are no awards given for the selfless labor that caregivers deliver, or for the emotional weight that providing extra care entails. Kim certainly earned a number of medals for being a road and health-care warrior and a solid partner in a battle that required perseverance, acts of kindness, physical endurance, diligence, and commitment. I would not have been able to do all that I did for those twelve years by myself.

I am also grateful for the many friends, agents, family associates, sponsors, and strangers who gave generous support in the days, months, and years of my need. It almost made the days and nights bearable. Still, with all that support, the heavy emotional toll, with hours, days, and months of energy expended just trying to survive, was exhausting.

It was a major chore to keep going through day after day of suffering. As anyone who has dealt with a chronic illness knows, it's a debilitating experience. I still marvel at how I managed to get through it without simply deciding to give up. I believe that my inner core—a mix of athlete, musician, and passionate life force—gave me the resilience of body, mind, and spirit to keep going. My sports-loving self found ways to turn the journey into a competitive game. How do you get through a tough game when you're not well, or down by twenty-five points? How do you deal with the hard reality of working against pain, oppression, racism, and prejudice for years and years? You go at it one moment, one play, one song, one day—or in my case, one shower, bath, or hospitalization at a time. It becomes a mission. You try to keep your eyes on the prize. The prize for me was that there might be a cure or some miracle one day down the road. But there were days when that miracle felt a million miles away.

I recall one day in 1999 when we were on tour in Alaska with friends, the musical duo Magpie, doing shows for young audiences at a theater in Anchorage. We were braving record-breaking double-digit cold temperatures and doing two shows and some community visits every day. We returned to our hotel room one afternoon and saw on the news that the football star Walter Payton had died of the same condition I had. I thought, "Oh my god, is that me in a few years?" After that sobering telecast, my companions helped me settle down and get through that moment as we tried to finish the tour, because as we all know, "the show must go on!"

That was the attitude and the reality that Kim and I held as we continued on. We couldn't afford to cancel a show, even as I got sicker and things became more difficult. Along the way, I tried every Western medical drug and every alternative approach available: acupuncture, acupressure, Reiki, massage, special diets, remote psychic healing, colonics, and just about any holistic or metaphysical protocol suggested by many well-meaning people. I learned to sort the advice and stay thankful that people cared so much.

There was one recommendation that did become a lifeline in the latter stages of my ordeal. On a Sunday night about eight or nine years into this journey, my body had a violent negative reaction to some supplements that a seemingly knowledgeable doctor had prescribed for me. I was in total body revolt and afraid that I wouldn't make it through the night. I looked around and found the name and number of an alternative healer that a friend had given me some months before, and in total desperation called the office at about 10:00 p.m. After listening to her voice message on the phone machine, I passionately began leaving a tearful message of my own. Midway through my delivery, this healer, a woman named Elsa Votava, mercifully picked up the phone. Speaking calmly in a very compassionate tone, she asked me several questions and then agreed to see me early that week. The first visit was very helpful, as she was able to use a number of healing protocols to get my body to settle down and return to functionality. Employing her expansive knowledge with a variety of techniques over time (including a measured number of chemical and natural supplements), she continued to work with me week after week, year after year, whenever I needed her. Right up to the day my liver failed completely, there were many occasions when she would literally pull me back from the brink of collapse and help me to keep going. Like all great healers, she showed a deep ability to listen and talk to me about what I was feeling in making her choices of treatment.

While I kept working through all of this liver toxicity, my judgement became impaired and wasn't always what it might have been. There were more than a few miraculous near misses, such as the time when, desperately needing a paycheck, Kim and I drove eight hours to do a gig at a middle school in Erie, Pennsylvania. Unbeknownst to me, I had so little blood in my body (I was bleeding internally from a related condition and getting biweekly blood transfusions) that all I could do that morning was sit on a stool on the stage and play the guitar as Kim sang and told our stories. I was unable to speak because words that formed in my head would fail to come out of my mouth except in gibberish when I tried to talk. Somehow, we got through the concert and then drove eight hours back home. By the time we arrived near home, I was so out of it that we went straight to a hospital emergency room where the ER doctor told me—in an angry rant following his initial exam—that he was stunned that I had not had a stroke. After another transfusion and some stabilizing medication, he said point blank, through pleading eyes, "You are never to do anything like this again!" It was advice that improved my future decision-making, and I was grateful for his passion and concern.

Finally, after more years of suffering, my liver deteriorated to the point where even Elsa couldn't rally me. It had nothing more to give, and as the damage took hold, I was in and out of hospitals in several states all through 2007 and 2008. The doctors at HUP had said that it would take about ten or twelve years for the disease to progress to the point of liver failure, and they were right. Elsa and others had bought me a little extra time, but in the summer of 2008 while we were on the road, the medical team at HUP wrote to say that testing indicated that I was now eligible for a liver transplant and that they were actively looking for donors. Kim and I were performing at the Summerfolk Music and Crafts Festival, a couple of hours north of Toronto, where I struggled through a weekend of musical performances with my body completely swollen and toxic. Following our Sunday afternoon performance at the festival, I was so weak that friends had to help me into the van that would drive us to the airport. They said later that they didn't expect to see me again.

Unfortunately, we did not go straight home. I tried my best to manage myself through another week of teaching at a music camp in New Hampshire, with my five-showers-and-two-baths-a-day-routine, but it was a near disaster. It boosted my spirits to be with our music community, but that late August week was a mental blur and a physical nightmare that ended in a late-night tearful goodbye to the WUMB Summer Acoustic Music Week camp staff and community and a long, disorienting ride home. Arriving at home, I saw the letter from HUP and it became clear that it was time to give up the fight. There would be no saving my liver, and it wasn't clear that they could save my life.

I was initially admitted to Ellis Hospital in Schenectady in mid-September 2008 and then transferred by van to Philadelphia, admitted, stabilized, and released, then re-admitted to the Hospital of the University of Pennsylvania about two weeks later after falling down a flight of stairs. September became October and I got sicker and sicker. I remember voting for Barack Obama's historic presidential election on an absentee ballot from my hospital bed with some cognitive difficulty, as the level of toxins from my compromised systems of elimination made even the smallest of tasks hard to negotiate. My friend, songwriter John Flynn, came to visit me often, and we watched the Phillies-Rays World Series games in my hospital room as I awaited word on whether a liver would become available. The hospital staff got used to our shouts and cheers, though I learned later from John that I had not been as boisterous and energetic in my cheering and high fives as my memory recalled. Still, there was a lot of momentary joy and celebration.

As I faced my uncertain fate, I had an epiphany. I had done a lot of emotional healing work with Elsa in those intervening years and had become aware that I had a lot of suppressed anger and hurt from the racism and prejudice I had experienced growing up as an African American in Philadelphia and from living in America. I thought about the taunts I had heard walking through neighborhoods and towns, North and South, where it was made clear I was not welcome. I thought about teachers, neighbors, bosses, coworkers, classmates, and teammates who were clearly racist or insensitive to the issue of injustice. I thought about the dangerous situations and all the trauma and microaggressions that I had faced and absorbed with quiet fortitude while touring around the country.

I also reflected on the examples of courage and strength that Jackie Robinson and others had demonstrated as trailblazers integrating major league baseball and other institutions. I thought about the courage of so many people of color who had endured oppression, personal sacrifice, and even death to pave my way. I vowed to myself that if I lived, I would speak out more fearlessly about issues of racism and intolerance. I resolved that I would make a difference.

I was near death and preparing to face what now seemed inevitable, but I had not lost hope. The reprieve came suddenly, late in the morning on October 28. A member of the transplant team came into my room and explained that a liver had been made available. A forty-three-year-old man had died in Delaware, and his liver was a perfect match. His family decided to donate his organs, and I would be one of five recipients who would benefit from their gracious generosity.

The liver arrived from Christiana Hospital in a Gift of Life Donor Program van that night, and the transplant procedure took place the next morning. It was a seven-hour operation that was described by my surgeon, Dr. Abraham Shaked, in the following way, "It was a beautiful liver. We put it in and it pinked right up!" Okay, pink is obviously good!

I had many waking dreams that focused on rebirth and life as the fog of anesthesia lifted to reveal that I was still on this side of the reality plain. And to make the whole thing even more fantastic, one of my nurses whispered in my ear, as I struggled to awaken (amid dreams of Phillies players past and present) that the losing-est team in baseball history, my Phillies, had actually won the World Series. Miracles truly do happen. On that day, there were two!

I was in the hospital for about ten days after the transplant. When I was finally released from the hospital, I felt like a free and grateful man. Although I was still quite weak, at least I was alive, with a new and promising chance to regain a life.

My post-transplant recovery was a hard, years-long process. At the beginning I didn't have the strength to hold my guitar, much less sing. I remember that about three weeks after I got out of the hospital, I was riding in the car with my brother-in-law Peter when James Taylor's song "Your Smiling Face" came on the radio. Without forethought, I heard the words "Whenever I see your smiling face, I have to smile myself" come spilling out of my mouth. When the singing came back, it came back with a vengeance. I couldn't stop singing. Music—so long distant from my thoughts and practice—brought my passion alive again.

After three months of recovery, still gradually regaining my strength, I began performing again, probably much too soon. I knew that I wanted to sing in a completely new and different way. The sound of chords and words had a depth and freedom that hit my ear with a new vibrancy. To get my bearings, I began to listen to the recordings Kim and I had made over the years to start remembering our songs and to reimagine how they could be played or sung differently. It took months to regain the lung capacity and the strength to deliver the phrasing in the ways my mind wanted to execute it. I was now singing with the passion and conviction of a man who had been given a second chance at life, and I intended to use it to the fullest.

To be honest, some days it all felt too big and overwhelming, this new life crashing in. My emotions were a roller coaster ride that dipped and swirled without warning. There is a complex psychological component of recovery as well as a physical one. After about a year, even though I was doing well physically, I found myself dragging through days of sadness and depression. I was struggling to find a perspective and balance that could keep me feeling grateful for this life-saving gift and the opportunities it now presented. With Kim away in New York working on her PhD for much of the time, I spent days and weeks alone at home trying to make sense of this new life with someone else's liver making my life possible. In addition to the mental confusion and loneliness, the necessities of life—shopping, cleaning, self-care, making meals, house maintenance, bills and medical debts, doctor visits, and the demands of reestablishing a career after so much time away—all began to crowd in and blot out the joy of simply being alive. Days turned into restless, angst-filled nights, with no clear path forward. I know now that I had sunk into a deep depression and I was spiraling.

One day while out in town looking for a birthday card for a friend, I walked into an art gallery and came upon a small figure of a turtle carved from a deer antler that seemed to call out to me from its case. Turtles are icons of longevity, stability, persistence, and patience. I asked to see it, and in an instant I felt like I had been connected to a source of energy and comfort that began to shift my mental framework. I quickly bought that little emblem, strung it on a chain, and started a ritual of putting it on every day as a reminder to recommit myself to a new sense of mission that, to this day, informs my life and my daily activity. Each day, by placing my turtle around my neck, I reconnect in gratitude with the gift I was given by the family of that man whose death made a new start possible for me. I resonate with the joy that people tell me they can hear in my music. Turtle (and now my second turtle talisman, "New Turtle") reminds me to try to walk in rhythm with the grace, compassion, and generosity of spirit that exists in our love and care for each other. It is an action that reminds me to share the blessings forward. It doesn't make every day magic or keep me from feeling challenged or overwhelmed at times. But it does remind me that I have a choice in how I see the things that come across my plate. And most often, it allows me some grace in deciding how to face them.

A couple years after the transplant, having regained my songwriting touch and feeling more settled, a song came to me in the days after Hurricane Irene had inflicted heavy damage and destruction across the New England states and in our town of Middleburgh, New York. I had traveled north to Toronto just after that devastating storm to meet with my friend Ken Whiteley about producing a CD with the new songs I'd written. We spent a few days doing pre-production work in his studio and, after reviewing, singing, playing through, and discussing eleven songs, he asked, "What are you going to call this CD?"

"My working title is 'Resurrection' or 'Resurrection Day,'" I replied.

Looking at the list of songs before him, he said, "There's no song here with that title."

"Yeah, I know," I said.

"Is there going to be one?"

In that moment, I had no ready answer, but I smiled and held the thought as we finished our work for the day. That night, alone in my room, I heard an opening chord sequence in my head and picked up my guitar. Then I quickly wrote this phrase on an empty page in my song journal: "You can open your heart to the rising sun 'cause it's alright. It's over!"

As I often do during song starts, I began to play that chord sequence over and over again while singing those words. Without warning, I immediately burst into tears and cried for a long while—as I'm doing now, writing this.

It was a very hard place to return to emotionally because that twelve-year journey of liver illness was by far the hardest thing I had ever experienced. But I let the emotions wash over me, and in the morning I had a couple of verses and that chorus. I told Ken, as he drove me to the train, that there would indeed be a title song. On the train, I wrote and wept and wrote and wept as the song took shape.

Arriving back in the US, I saw the damage that Hurricane Irene had visited on my home area and I realized that what I was writing about resurrection had multiple implications. Seeing the devastation in my rural New York county and envisioning the rebuilding that would be needed also primed the writing pump. My illness and transplant had been my personal hurricane, and the sun did rise again after twelve terrible years of sorrow. In time, it would also rise in the communities of my adopted home.

Writing the song "Resurrection Day"—trying to capture in words my experience of getting progressively more ill until I was on the brink of death and then being miraculously brought back to life—was a very deep and challenging process. It became the title song of an album that Kim and I released in 2012. The song is so filled with emotion for me that when I perform it, I have to do so through an emotional filter that I've developed to keep myself from breaking down in tears. If I open that door, it is like opening the floodgates.

As I write this chapter from the vantage point of being close to my fourteenth post-transplant anniversary, I can say that as difficult as it was, the whole experience of illness and my return to health has turned out to be a remarkable spiritual journey. It gave me reasons and time to face myself and to process years of emotional pain that I had pushed down into the recesses of my body and mind. I undertook an honest assessment of who I was and what I wanted to keep as part of me and what I needed to let go. I was challenged to acknowledge my fears, rage, and wounds, but I also learned where I had strengths that I was not using to the fullest— gifts that I could allow to rise and blossom. It also freed my voice and boosted my willingness to take more risks in music and in life and to be a more direct actor in relationships and performances. It gave me a new language to use in writing and in speaking my thoughts to the world.

Before long, I realized that having come to a new sense of self, I no longer carried the tension in my body that had been there since childhood—a feeling that would well up inside me in moments of stress or uncertainty. The donation of an organ was the gift that saved my life in multiple ways. I woke up from that seven-hour operation with a chance to live and chase my dreams anew. (And the chance to savor doughnuts, although I do that only rarely these days.)

I do not know the identity of the donor, but I wrote a letter to his family to express my gratitude for the incredible gift of life he gave me. I never got a response, but that's alright. I can pay his gift forward. And I try to do that every day through my music, my work in schools, and my work with the Living Legacy Project. I do indeed have a new song to sing.

Please sign up to be an organ donor and encourage your loved ones to do so too.

Resurrection Day

You can open your heart to the rising sun
Cause it's all right . . . it's over!
Been a long, long journey, but now that's done
And it's all right . . . it's over.
Remember how you cried, "Just one more day!"
The pain so deep inside that all you could say
Will I get over? Can I get over?

The story unfolds on your weary face
But that's all right . . . it's over!
Somehow you made it though,
You found the grace to say it's all right . . . it's over!

The light is shining now for all to see
The pain is fading

You can set your heart free
Now that it's over. . . You know it's over.

Chorus:

You can raise your voice and let the angels sing.
You can rise right up and learn to spread your wings!
Hallelujah! A new day is here
You've got a new race to run
Resurrection day. . . Resurrection day
Resurrection day . . . Resurrection day!
You are rising. It's all right . . . it's over!

CHAPTER FOURTEEN

HICKORY HILL

Hickory Hill. Such an innocuous, even pleasant-sounding name for a place where the horrors of slavery subjugated my ancestors and more than two hundred other unfortunate souls. My great-great-great-grandmother Bibhanna was enslaved on a plantation of that name, and her forced relational physical encounters with either her owner, William Fanning Wickham, or his son, Williams Carter Wickham of Ashland, Virginia, resulted in six children who are my forebears. Coming to terms with the fact that the Wickham family both owned and provides one half of my lineage has been no easy task.

I learned of this unsettling—but not uncommon—history of my family's beginnings in America at a family reunion in Richmond, Virginia, in July 1992. At the request of relatives in Virginia, many of us from Maryland, Pennsylvania, and New Jersey drove south for a rare but well-planned reunion. There, in a hotel on the outskirts of Richmond, about three hundred members of the Hewlett kin group gathered to meet relatives, most of whom we had met or seen only once or twice when we were younger, or had simply heard about in family tales. To my mother, aunts, and uncles, however, this was a grand homecoming. Our gathering of cousins by the dozens quickly turned into a joyful, nonstop, raucous routine of "Come over here! You gotta meet your cousin Bunky from Culpepper and his wife and kids! Give them all a hug!" We met people day and night and hugged until our arms were numb.

The gathering began on Friday evening and lasted through Sunday afternoon with a church service at the Providence Baptist Church in Ashland, Virginia, twenty-five miles north of Richmond, where we knew the family had deep roots. Saturday afternoon was especially exciting, as Kim and I sang a short program of spirituals. Afterwards, one of our cousins, Kaye E. Bush-Gray, an enthusiastic teacher from Richmond, regaled the family for about two hours, sharing the details of a special project that she had been working on for some time. Kaye revealed that, inspired by the book and television presentation *Roots*, she had been researching our family genealogy. As she began to speak, she instructed some of our young relatives from Virginia to distribute booklets containing her research. Soon we were all holding a meticulously prepared document that told the story of our family, the Hewletts.

Kaye revealed that our family began on the plantation in Ashland, Virginia, called Hickory Hill. Like so many other African American families, ours started with a union (it certainly was not a marriage or anything resembling an equal exchange of love or power) between a master and a slave. Our ancestor Bibhanna was a single young woman, the daughter of an enslaved couple, trafficked from the West Indies, owned by a prominent master, William Fanning Wickham. Born on the plantation in the early 1800s, she was working as an enslaved field hand. In 1833, Bibhanna gave birth to the first of six children. At this point, the research is inconclusive as to whether these six children were fathered by William Fanning

Wickham or his son, Williams Carter Wickham. Both men also fathered children with their wives.

The Wickhams were considered one of the first families of Virginia. William Fanning Wickham was a lawyer, wealthy landowner, and master of Hickory Hill. Williams Carter Wickham would go on to serve in the Civil War and became a high-ranking officer in the Confederate Army, a brigadier general in the cavalry of Northern Virginia. He also served in the Virginia State Senate and the Confederate Congress. After the war, he was vice president of the Chesapeake and Ohio Railroad from 1869 until his death in 1888.

Bibhanna, my great-great-great grandmother, lived on the plantation until her death after the war. Though she was not married to the father of her children, the union between her and whichever Wickham sired her children makes them my great-great-great grandparents. This news, while not entirely shocking, was a monumental revelation to the family at a time when most African Americans, prior to the internet and research organizations like Ancestry.com, had no real idea of their family's beginnings or a sense of place and legacy.

After the initial mental jolt of that revelation, I felt over-whelmed by a mix of emotions. Feelings of pain, anger, sadness, and some gratitude for knowing the truth swirled around inside of me. These facts put my existence in a new context but added no real closure to my family's enslaved past.

In the years following the reunion, I didn't come to any real sense of peace about how I wished to share this story with the world. I mostly kept it to myself until the summer of 2010, when I was teaching at the Swannanoa Gathering near Asheville, North Carolina. The Gathering is an annual music camp for adults that runs every summer on the campus of Warren Wilson College. It was my second year on the faculty and I was there to teach two courses, one on vocal and stage performance and one on the songs and stories of the Underground Railroad. The second class was a singing-intensive course that illustrated how song relates to culture and the history of slavery and race in America. I was blessed with two very engaged groups of students, both eager to dive into our spirited sessions with passion and curiosity.

On Wednesday afternoon in the spirituals course, I had planned to share lots of songs and background information illustrating how spirituals like "Wade in the Water," "Go Down Moses," "Steal Away to Jesus," and others were used to build relationship and inspire determination in the enslaved community, while also creating a viable means of resistance and escape. ("Wade in the Water," one of the pivotal code songs used for escape, is my favorite song in the world.) It made for a lively session, with lots of singing and questions. The class was so energized that we cruised rather quickly through the material I'd planned for the day, and with thirty minutes left in the scheduled class period, I began to realize that I would need to add some additional stories or songs to fill out our time.

Not wanting to edge into my next day's lesson plan, and knowing that ending early wasn't an option, my thoughts turned to that family story that I'd been carrying around for years. I wasn't sure that I could get all of the details right, but if I could, it was the perfect thing to add to give some context to our earlier discussion about the complex nature of the relationships between masters and the enslaved during the time of slavery.

I told the story of Bibhanna and the Wickham family as best I could, and the class was fascinated. We launched into a discussion about Thomas Jefferson and Sally Hemmings and talked about other stories that touched on the complex racial relationships that have gone unacknowledged for years in American culture. After singing one last song, I dismissed the class and considered the episode over. But one of my students, Fran A. Oates, herself a storyteller, came up to engage me in conversation.

"So, you say that your family is related to the Wickhams of Richmond?"

"That's what my cousin's research tells us," I replied.

She smiled and said, "Well, I grew up knowing the Wickham family. As a matter of fact, one of the daughters, Lisa, was one of my best friends when I was a teenager. I haven't thought of her in thirty years, but that's an amazing story. I think it's worth looking her up. If I were to find her, would you be interested in making contact?"

My mind was spinning, but I said what I thought was the right answer.

"Why, sure! That would be great!" In my head I can remember thinking, "You don't mean that." It was just something to say. Besides, what were the odds that after all this time, she would be able to find Lisa and follow up to connect us?

As they say, be careful what you ask for! A year went by and I hadn't given that conversation any thought when I got an email from Fran with the news that her search for Lisa had been successful. Lisa was now back living in Richmond, and they had enjoyed a wonderful reunion.

"I told her the story you shared with us, and she wants to

talk to you! She runs a business and works from home and said you can call her any day."

I froze as I read her email. This connection, once so distant over history and time, was now a very real thing. And this wasn't someone else's history—it was mine. The ball was now in my court, and I wasn't sure I wanted to pick it up.

I spent two long weeks thinking about what a conversation might sound like if I were to pick up the phone and make that call. In most of the scenarios I played in my head, it did not play out very well. But finally, my thoughts turned to what felt like a responsibility to my work, to my family, to my past, and to my personal credo in life to try to face the truth whenever I find it, no matter how awkward or scary it might seem. I had presented hundreds upon hundreds of performances about slavery and its impact on American society, and now I had a chance to engage it on a personal level in a way that many historians and citizens can only dream of.

That call had to be made.

I gathered my courage, picked up the phone and dialed the number. Two rings later a voice answered, and I haltingly said, "Hi! My name is Reggie Harris, and I . . ." Before I could get another word out, the female voice on the other end said, almost accusingly but with a friendly tone, "Where've you been?"

I tried to respond. "Oh, well, I travel a lot, and my life is kind of busy and complicated . . ." But Lisa pushed in.

"You were supposed to call me two weeks ago!"

"Well, this is the first chance I had to actually call you," I lied.

"I understand that we are related? We're cousins?" she said.

"Well, yes," I replied, figuring that her next question would be "So what proof do you have?"

But Lisa took a different tack. "How old are you?" she asked.

"Fifty-nine," I answered.

She laughed. "Well, if we are cousins, then I'm two years older than you and that means I can boss you around!"

The ice was broken. We both laughed. And then we went on to have a spirited conversation for two hours. It was the first of many conversations that we would share, reuniting as distant family, sharing honest reflections and facts about our lives.

We became willing partners on a journey that would land us both on the property at Hickory Hill, walking the land together in an awkward and surreal afternoon two years later. Although the land is no longer a plantation, it was chilling for me to be there. Thinking about Bibhanna and my other forebears enduring the cruelties of slavery in that place made it a challenge to be walking there with Lisa. My song "Hickory Hill" came out of our visit to the property.

"Hickory Hill"

Barren fields to the horizon
The ghosts of autumn catch the wind
Memories of those saints and sinners
Gather round to haunt us once again.
Now we are finally here together
Standing silent, face to face
Secret family undercover
Born of shame, saved by hope and grace.

Hickory Hill, we're on hallowed ground
Walkin' side by side, wondering what we've found
Hearts break open wide
Across the great divide
I can see the questions in your eyes
Now that we are home again.

They celebrate the grand illusion
And they write it up for all to see
But in that mystery of confusion
There lies a truth that might one day set us free.
So now our stories come together
Across these fields of broken dreams
And the blood that binds us all together
Is indeed much thicker than it seems.

Hickory Hill, we're on solid ground
Standin' side by side, wondering what we've found
Hearts break open wide
Across the great divide
Can you hear the demons as they die
Now that we are home again?

Since that day in 2010 when Lisa and I first spoke, I have slowly met other members of the Wickham family and formed relationships with my White cousins. Lisa's older sister Wallis was the first Wickham that I met in person. Lisa shared the details of our initial phone call with Wallis, who then came to a performance of mine in January 2011 at a school in the Arlington, Massachusetts, school district where she worked as the

Associate Superintendent of Schools. After the show we met, hugged, and had lunch. The next year, in November 2012, I made it to Richmond and met Lisa, her brother George, and his wife Mary for dinner and an overnight at her home. Later, I would meet George and Mary's son Clayton when he sought me out at a concert performance in New York City. We enjoyed a spirited get-to-know-you chat that night, and he and I have since found a thought-provoking connection as he continues to work, in his words, "at making sense of things that don't make sense about my place in the world." He shared with me that he longs for closure on the difficult issues that were not discussed in his childhood growing up as a White boy in the South. His dad George has offered some similar thoughts in our conversations.

Over the past twelve years, there have been many moments of personal connection between me and various members of the Wickham family. During our first conversation in December 2010, Lisa expressed regret that her family history contained the owning of slaves. She was quick to mention, partly in jest, that she had gone door to door to campaign for President Barack Obama, which I laughingly dismissed as "Too little, too late!" She also mentioned that as a child she always believed that her family had owned slaves but was upset that she and her siblings could not get the older adults to talk about it. She mentioned that Wallis used to give their father, Henry, a very hard time in discussions about that time period, and about his role in supporting segregation as a lawyer representing the state following the *Brown v. Board of Education* court ruling requiring racial integration in schools in the 1950s and '60s.

On one of my subsequent visits to Richmond, Lisa, Wallis, George, Mary, and I went to Monroe Park in Richmond to stand before the statue of Williams Carter Wickham. As we stood there, all of the members of the Wickham family expressed regret about this difficult family history and wondered what to do with it. I found myself at a loss for words, grateful yet numb in the moment. We spent the weekend in an emotional limbo, being kind and conversive, yet unable to put words to the emotions that were clearly present in us all.

Then on Monday, while Wallis was waiting for Lisa to take her to the airport for her return to Boston, Wallis and I shared a very personal moment sitting alone in Lisa's kitchen. We talked quietly about the events of the weekend, obviously working to have some closure. In that moment, Wallis turned to me and apologized for "what my family did to your family." It was a very poignant moment that both of us have acknowledged several times since that day.

Lisa and I decided to take the opportunity later in that same visit to find the Richmond Slavery Reconciliation Statue, which is located near Richmond's former slave market in Shockoe Bottom, about 100 yards from the Main Street station of Amtrak. My friend Greg Greenway had told me about its existence a few years before and mentioned that he would love to go to see it with me sometime. Before Lisa and I made our visit, I called Greg to tell him that we were going to make the journey. He was thrilled and asked when we planned to go. I told him that we would go before I was scheduled to board a train for Philadelphia at 6:00 p.m., two days from that night. There was a silence on the phone and then he said, "I'll be there!"

Knowing that he was on tour, I asked, "Where are you?"

"Chicago!"

"You're driving?" (Greg hates to fly.)

"Yes, but I'll be there. I can't miss this."

And two days later, having made a wild fifteen-hour, 900-mile drive, he was!

Greg was born and raised in Richmond. Starting in childhood, he was acutely aware of the racism and prejudice that permeated the region and his own family, as well his family's history of slave ownership. Greg and I have acknowledged the need to recognize the power of these historic sites and monuments in our national memory, and the need to have time to let healing take root in our hearts and minds. It was only right that he be there to meet Lisa as we did the same.

On our drive to the monument that afternoon, after a weekend of stirring up our emotional trauma, Lisa turned to me and asked, "Do you ever really think about the fact that you have Wickham blood in you?"

"No!" I blurted out. Partly in jest, but with a ring of truth.

"Well, you do!" she countered.

I waited to respond, feeling the slight but present tension of the moment. "Yeah, I know."

We found a parking spot (not an easy thing to do given the congestion near the station) and walked to the spot. The memorial is tucked away under Interstate 95 and all of the commerce that has built up in the area. Crossing the street, we stood in front of the Richmond Slavery Reconciliation statue, a fifteen-foot-high statue of two figures embracing. We silently took in the contrast between this relatively small monument to the 300,000 people who were brought ashore in Richmond in bondage and sold into lives of demeaning slavery and the multiple sixty-foot-high statues of Confederate veterans placed along Monument Avenue in Richmond, installed as iconic statements of purpose by the Daughters of the Confederacy.

Within minutes Greg arrived. We hugged, I introduced him to Lisa, and they hugged. And then we stood together, once again engaging our hearts and minds in that now familiar but painful struggle of trying to make sense of it all.

After that amazing November day in 2012, I had shared the news of my walk with Lisa at Hickory Hill almost immediately with my sister Marlene and my first cousin Valorie. Since I had taken pictures of the property and of us walking together that day, it was an easy story to relate at our Thanksgiving gathering. They loved the pictures, and we talked about the history as we knew it from the reunion. Marlene and Valorie were intrigued about the contact, as were my Aunt Sweetsie and Uncle Henry, the remaining elders of my family. While my immediate family members expressed mild interest in finding a time to get together and meet the Wickhams, years went by with no push from any of them to do so.

In July 2016, my friend and colleague Annette Marquis at the Living Legacy Project invited me to present our family story at the First Unitarian Universalist Church of Richmond where she serves as a worship leader. I asked George Wickham, a teacher, if he would share the dais with me in a service that became titled "Family Revealed: A Conversation." In the end, both Lisa and George joined me to share our family story in that Sunday morning service. During the service Lisa, who had originally not planned to be on stage, shared that part of her great sorrow and anger was that our shared ancestor Williams Carter Wickham had violated a woman's body who was not his wife and who he essentially "owned." George shared his difficulty of coming to some sense of peace as a White male Southerner with his legacy and privilege.

In the summer of 2019, Clayton and I had a reflective conversation over lunch in Michigan, where he was completing his student teaching as part of his graduate school studies. At one point in our lunch conversation, having discussed our growing connection and how it had produced some complicated thoughts and challenges in his approach to material he was required to teach, he looked at me and in a very calm and thoughtful voice said, "I know why my family wants to know you. Why do you want to know us?"

I was dumbstruck. I paused and smiled. "You know, Clayton, I'm still trying to sort that out!"

I got the opportunity to do just that a few weeks later when George and Wallis invited me to take part in the Wickham family summer gathering at a camping resort in Holderness, New Hampshire. For a delightful and fascinating three days, fifteen of us spent time relaxing, eating together, hiking, talking, singing, and questioning. There were some puzzled looks from the other residents of the camp, among whom there were no other people of color present, other than one groundskeeper. I was twice mistaken for being a member of the staff. On a two-hour history-focused tour of Squam Lake, the boat captain watched us—fourteen white people and me—interacting and finally asked me, when I got close enough, "So how do you know these folks?

"They're my cousins!"

Wide-eyed silence, then laughter. "Whoa! There's a story there, I'll bet."

"Yup. It's a long one. And we're still writing it."

It was a time of becoming more family than "examiners of historical connection." It has deepened the well.

In October 2019, Wallis, her husband Dan Raemer, George, and Mary all came to experience a civil rights pilgrimage on a tour with the Living Legacy Project where I was a trip leader. Wallis recruited several of her friends to join us on the journey. While we didn't choose to formally acknowledge each other as family to the other participants, many on the bus already knew of our history and asked questions privately during the week. We traveled to sites of civil unrest, protests, lynching memorials, and human triumphs in Alabama, Mississippi, and Tennessee and found that our attention to these civil rights stories made aspects of our personal familial connections to this history more vibrant. The Wickham/Raemers and I took the opportunity to share a number of moments, in pairs or as a group, to check in with each other for conversation and reflection. Since that trip we have found more chances to reflect, each in our way, on how our family history resonates in our everyday lives.

Over time, I have heard from Wallis slightly more than I have from other family members, though a scroll through my archived emails reveals a robust trail of conversations, articles, and even a few comments from Mason, the one sister I have yet to meet in person. There is one very lively thread of emails in 2017 that chronicled the fallout that occurred when Clayton and his brother Will wrote a letter to the *Richmond Times-Dispatch* and the Richmond City Council to advocate, as descendants of General Wickham, for the removal of Confederate monuments from public lands in Richmond. Their letter reached the front page of the paper and garnered comments from several public officials and from some very angry citizens who questioned whether the young men (not the term they used) were even related to the general.

In July 2020 that advocacy would resurface, as both Clayton and Will took to the streets to join thousands of citizens in Richmond and elsewhere during that intense summer that felt like a great awakening of many Americans to the ongoing pervasiveness of police violence and brutality against Black bodies. In that cauldron of protest, the statue of Williams Carter Wickham was toppled, along with other confederate monuments around Richmond and throughout the country. Though not among the crowd of people who toppled the statue, neither Clayton nor Will were sorry to see it fall. Those events led to Clayton, Wallis, and I being interviewed by reporters from the *New York Times* and to an interview with Don Lemon on the CNN podcast *Silence Is Not an Option*. Our family story also gained a prominent spot in a chapter of Don Lemon's 2021 book, *This Is the Fire*.

In writing this book, I began to think more about the healing that might be possible between the Black and White branches of my family tree. I spoke further about it with my sister Marlene and my Hewlett cousins, and as a result, we arranged two virtual reunions with members on both sides which went very well. (Due to Covid, we couldn't meet in person.) Relationships are starting to form among more members of my Hewlett family and the Wickhams, and more are coming. Lisa and Marlene became text buddies.

In the late summer of 2020, my cousin George Wickham came to spend a long weekend with me in Middleburgh to help with some projects around the house. To my surprise, he completely rebuilt the crumbling old pump shed on my rural property, making a gift of the expense and time. I was amazed at his carpentry skills! The visit gave us time to talk, commiserate, and laugh as we continue our embrace of this remarkable relationship. Wallis and I are scheduled to do some shared programs together in the coming year, sharing our perspectives on this American narrative with willing audiences.

At times, I need to keep myself from drifting into thoughts that this history is more important to me than it is to the Wickhams. That's probably a personal and racial battle that is part of the struggle I face in dealing with the various aspects of White privilege. White people, regardless of their attitude or commitment to issues of race, simply don't have to think about them or their consequences every day. They always have the option, as the cultural default, to relax, fail to notice, or even walk away. But my emails from Wallis, Lisa, and George and our more recent conversations reveal that our connection has brought them a very deep passion, some life-transforming clarity, and clear joy. Those emails also reveal an ongoing struggle that we share in dealing with the echoes of the past and its ramifications in a nation still being shaped and tormented by race, privilege, and oppression.

Perhaps the most wonderful development that has resulted from my meeting the Wickhams and their getting to know me is the creation of a scholarship fund by the Wickham family called the Wickham-Hewlett Scholarship for Racial Justice. It came about as a result of discussions about accountability among the Wickhams. The scholarship will help first-generation college students with demonstrated financial need who are enrolled at one of Virginia's twenty-three community colleges to pursue an associate degree or workforce certification. Special consideration will be given to students from underserved communities and those who are committed to working on racial justice in Black and Brown communities. This forward-thinking act on the part of the Wickhams, which grew out of our mutual openness to getting to know each other and several years of shared dialogue and experiences, is a beautiful example of the healing and bridge-building that can be done by White allies. It fuels my hope.

I can truthfully say that my Wickham family lineage is now an integral part of my embrace of my heritage and continues to fuel my mission in music and in life, while at the same time I continue to reckon with multiple truths and emotions. Grief, anger, curiosity, gratitude, and an openness to forgiveness jostle for position in my head and my heart. As I open myself to further bridge-building work, I find out more about myself and my own need for healing.

As I reflect on the emotional and spiritual journey I have been on with regards to the Wickhams, I find that these words from Rabbi Yael Levy capture my inner work and my intention: "to encourage the heart to risk vulnerability, seek truth, and shine with courage and compassion for the sake of each other and all the world."

CHAPTER FIFTEEN

DEEPER THAN THE SKIN

After Kim and I separated in 2016, I longed to do something more specifically focused on inviting Americans into conversations about race, prejudice, and White privilege in order to bridge the great divide between the races. I wanted to lean into my life experience as a Black man in America and my identity as a musician, educator, and cultural ambassador. Highlighting the true American history that many people have denied, or of which they are blissfully and dangerously unaware, would have to be part of that work.

Scientific research tells us that human beings are hardwired for story and song. My belief was that sharing personal stories and songs would make this history more accessible and might inspire more communities to embrace the hard work of finding connection and unity. To that end, in the last several years I have taken on projects that have allowed me to engage with people around racial healing in more visceral and impactful ways. The first is my involvement as co-president and musical director of the Living Legacy Project, an organization that takes people on four- and eight-day civil rights pilgrimages through the South.

The second is a presentation that my good friend and fellow musician Greg Greenway and I created in 2016 called

Deeper Than the Skin. As friends for more than thirty years, Greg and I have shared many expansive conversations about history, race, culture, music, sports, and justice. Born just three days apart in December 1952, our lives began on different sides of the historical and racial divide, with me a Black descendant of Bibhanna who was enslaved on the Hickory Hill plantation and Greg a White descendent of slave owners, born and raised in the capital of the confederacy—Richmond, Virginia. Our Virginia origins are separated by only a few miles of geography but a universe of history and life experiences.

From a very early age, Greg had noticed and begun to struggle with the legacy of Southern racism and his own family's history of slave ownership. He was acutely aware of the ways in which the cauldron of race in America weighed on his family, his neighbors, his schoolmates, his basketball teammates, his hometown, and the nation. That struggle has been a very deep part of shaping our friendship. I knew that I had found a powerful ally in this White male musician who cares just as deeply about healing the racial divide in this country as I do. Our shared struggle is both personal and global.

Greg and I had talked numerous times about the importance of acknowledging historically traumatic events as a first step toward healing. To begin the journey of healing and recovery, we visited important sites of the civil rights struggle around the county. Our journey took us to hallowed places that are central to our nation's troubled legacy of injustice: the National Civil Rights Museum in Memphis, Tennessee; the site of the original Jamestown, Virginia, colony and the first known slave quarters just north of that site; the Edmund Pettus Bridge in Selma, Alabama (the site of the Bloody Sunday attack on peaceful protesters during the modern civil rights movement); and the Whitney Plantation and Slavery Museum in Wallace, Louisiana, on the banks of the Mississippi River west of New Orleans. It was one of the many thousands of places at which the nation's economic wealth was built on the backs of enslaved Africans, just like Hickory Hill. Steeping ourselves in these places of historical oppression helped us prepare ourselves to use our own personal stories to shed light on the underlying tensions that have divided Americans and on a way forward to reconciliation.

Our goal with the Deeper Than the Skin presentation is to educate, inform, and hopefully inspire people to take a risk and become part of a growing new community of antiracists. We believe that the best way to do this is not to stand in front of people and give them facts and figures, but to share our stories—not as experts, but simply as two "brothers" who have found in each other a kindred passion to reduce the level of animosity, hate, and fear in our country. Personal stories connect us to the deepest parts of who we are as a human family. Coming together to acknowledge our own and others' particular narratives can help us move toward racial healing.

It can be a hard thing to repeatedly look into the faces of audiences that are coming to this challenge for the very first time, to stand and tell my story about being a Black man in America and to have them ask the most basic questions again and again. That conversation and the reflections that surround it are not easy to express, coming as they do from a place much deeper than the skin. But I believe it is essential for us as Americans to have these conversations because as citizens of this nation we are all connected.

And as strong an ally as Greg is, even inside the trust of our friendship we know that there will be moments when we find ourselves living into the cracks and uncertain spaces of our very different life narratives. One such moment surfaced on a Deeper Than the Skin tour through North Carolina in 2019. As we negotiated an audience Q&A following a performance, a woman stood to express her appreciation for our willingness to stand together in public. She said, "I applaud you for the courage that each of you show in doing this in such a volatile climate."

Taking the first turn to respond, Greg replied, "Thank you very much. But I don't see this as something that requires courage. It's just the right thing to do."

In that moment, I felt the gulf between our personal realities widen as I realized once again that Greg was speaking from the safety and comfort of his White privilege. Unlike mine, his lived experience did not make him fearful about the potential dangers inherent in our delivering our message. I also realized that I had not been sharing my own rising levels of anxiety with him as news of increasing racial hostility and attacks spread around the nation. An incident of random targeting by a hate group or an individual like Dylann Roof could easily be possible at any one of our performances. To that end, I countered Greg's answer with my own.

"Thank you, Ma'am. And pardon my brother Greg's honest sense of resolve. But I don't believe he is aware of just how easy it would be for our message to draw fire from the many people who are feeding on this current climate of hate. I try not to focus on it, but I know that we are potentially in danger every time we take the stage, and I'm grateful for your acknowledgement. Greg's right, it is the right thing to do, but it's courageous too. Greg and I will be having a chat about that later, as we often do." And we did.

Another chat had been necessary after Greg and I made a visit to see Randy Hughes, one of the finest guitar luthiers in the business, to have him play doctor to our ailing Martin guitars. We were on tour in separate cars so Greg, having been to the shop before, suggested I just follow him. He told me nothing about the route or the distance to the destination. Twenty minutes or so after we exited the highway, I figured that we were only a few turns away from our destination. We had been in a somewhat populated commercial area, but after several more minutes I found that we were twisting and turning down one heavily wooded rural road after another, each feeling more isolated than the last. We were passing backcountry shacks and signs of the confederacy and gun ownership, and I had no sense of where I was. My mind began to replay scenes from *Deliverance* and chases of civil rights workers. I heard voices in my brain screaming, "Turn around, Black man! Go back while you still can!"

I still trusted that Greg wouldn't intentionally take me into a situation that would cause me harm, but I have had more than enough experiences of insensitivity to know that White folks don't always see danger where race is concerned before it rears its ugly head. Just about the time I was contemplating some evasive action, we came roaring up one last hill and into a clearing where I saw Randy's beautiful house and workshop.

I shakily got out of the car, took a measured breath, and surprised Greg with an expletive. "Couldn't you have told me how deep in the woods this is?" I nearly shouted at him. "Do you have any idea what I'm feeling right now?"

He didn't. And so we had a chat.

America is a country in which narratives collide. The myths of our nation's founding are so strong that the truth of how we came to be where we are as a country is not universally known. The story of African Americans prior to 1776 and before America's birth as a nation has been under-told. In fact, we are a nation founded on oppression and slavery of many kinds, all of which we have been encouraged—almost commanded—to ignore, until it leaks or explodes into violence and hatred.

Educating people about the unvarnished history of systematic American racism—and the story of the struggle and perseverance of Black people to overcome it—has become an integral part of my life and career. While it can be deeply depressing and enraging to see how easily the progress gained through years of hard struggle can be thwarted by the concerted actions of politicians, media pundits, and citizens determined to sabotage it with misinformation and clever pandering to base emotions, it has also been deeply rewarding to do this work as a way to give back to those brave and ingenious souls who paved the way for us. Those who waded through the dark waters of slavery and the Jim Crow era truly "made a way outta no way," as the old folks would say. It has been gratifying to see people of all ages, races, and backgrounds become awakened to the importance and relevance of that hidden history.

While we don't connect with everyone ("They're just trying to make us feel bad about our ancestors," I heard one woman mutter under her breath after a performance), it is encouraging to witness the positive actions that arise from our presentations. People follow up in multiple ways. Many visit the Deeper Than the Skin website, where we have a list of books and resources for fuller engagement and understanding. People also sign up for further contact or relate some personal story that they didn't share in person. Some people announce the start of book clubs or racial equity conversation circles in their communities. Others choose to sponsor a show in their local schools as curriculum enhancement. We encourage those who want to dive deeper to seek out opportunities for antiracism training or prejudice reduction workshops. Our presentations have inspired letter-writing campaigns to legislators and voter registration drives. I've also been invited to work with teachers and artists in residence in several states to further the work.

Emails we receive after our presentation let us know that the program is having an impact:

I have been teaching for 35+ years, and I know when outsiders to a school community connect (or don't) with teenagers. Greg and Reggie connected. What they were able to bring to our students and faculty was a rich story of understanding, forthrightness, and integrity. They demonstrated in their storytelling just how important it is to be able to walk in the shoes of others who come from a world unlike your own. They also showed how important it is to remember that we are all part of the human community and that being able to reach out to one another, to be able to listen and empathize, is the essence of creating unity rather than division.

—J. A.

In our often-divided town, Deeper than the Skin brought together a diverse audience and served as a starting point for future conversation and action. It was amazing to be in the room where hundreds of people from many backgrounds deeply engaged the topic. They were lifted by the spirit of the music and made thought-provoking comments during the dialogue portion. People continue to talk about the concert weeks later.

—J. S. and A. B.

An audience member once came up to me after the show and said, "I almost didn't come here tonight. I've been so frustrated, angry, and upset by everything in the news. I really didn't want to leave the house. But when I saw the announcement of this program, I went online and I looked at your Facebook and webpage and what I saw gave me a little bit of hope. Your music spoke to me tonight, and I'm so glad I came."

After a recent show with Greg at the Chautauqua Institute in upstate New York, a man came to the microphone during the Q&A and said, "I'm an eighty-year-old White man from Richmond, Virginia. I came to your show today figuring that I would stay for five or ten minutes and leave to go to another event I was interested in. As you can see, I'm still here. What you shared today brought me to tears several times and you touched my heart. For that I deeply thank you."

At the end of one of my solo performances in Hennicker, New Hampshire, in August 2021, an older White couple came up to say, "We loved your show. Your stories touched us both deeply and we are so happy we were here to see you. We had no idea we would learn so much from your music. Do come again!" As they stepped away, my sponsor said, "Those are two of our most ardent Republicans in town. They've never approached an artist we've presented like this. I think you broke through something tonight."

If these words were spoken to me by just one person, that would be a marvelous thing. But I've heard similar statements from many people in state after state over the last few years, at intermission and at the end of shows as people go off into the night. They illustrate how music and dialogue in which we reveal our vulnerabilities can heal, transform, and make change possible. Music can unlock the hidden fears and misconceptions that keep mouths closed and boundaries in place.

Our society is a fabric woven from many different-colored threads. The idea is not to ignore the differences or become a colorblind society. The goal is to see the humanity in each other and appreciate the different lived experiences that make up our national fabric. Hope comes from a belief that we may yet learn to value unity and community above fear and division. As Malcolm X said in his late-in-life appeal to humanity, "We need more light about each other."

CHAPTER SIXTEEN

THE LIVING LEGACY PROJECT

I still remember the conversation that brought me to the Living Legacy Project back in 2010. I was teaching two music courses that summer for an annual weeklong gathering of Unitarian Universalists called the Southeastern Unitarian Universalist Summer Institute. A longtime friend of mine, Unitarian Universalist minister Rev. Dr. Hope Johnson (who sadly passed away in December 2020), sought me out on Friday afternoon and asked if I would be willing to provide some music for a worship service she was leading that night. It was obvious to me that she was on fire to share a new story in her life. She told me that she and her twin sister Janice Marie Johnson had just returned from an incredible experience on a journey to civil rights sites in the South. Hope and Janice Marie are originally from Jamaica and have lived extraordinary lives that have taken them all over the world. She confessed that this was the first time she had ever toured through the Southern United States, and she beamed about how transformational the experience had been.

"I never wanted to go there, given all that horrible history," she related. "But my talk tonight will be a recounting of that trip, and I'll be highly recommending this experience to everyone. It was with a group called Living Legacy."

But there was one aspect of the civil rights experience that she missed during the journey. "It didn't include any of the music, the spirituals and freedom songs, that fueled the civil rights movement. That would have really made it complete."

Knowing that the era and its music are passions of mine, Hope asked if I might have any interest in going on the next journey, scheduled for that fall, as a musician and historian. I said I might be interested if I was free.

The Living Legacy pilgrimage that she described grew out of the passion of a White Unitarian Universalist minister, Rev. Gordon Gibson, who, like hundreds of other clergy, had answered the call of Rev. Dr. Martin Luther King Jr. to come to Selma, Alabama, after the horrific events of Bloody Sunday in 1965. In that cauldron of hate and resistance, he joined with others in protests, marches, and community building projects. Later, Gordon served churches in Jackson and Ellisville, Mississippi, where he and his wife Judy spent years as White allies in that highly charged environment, working to overcome racism and injustice. After moving back North, they began leading trips to the South with the goal of helping people understand what history teaches about the work that still needs to be done in civil and human rights. To further this mission, they formed a partnership with Rev. Dr. Hope Johnson, Janice Marie Johnson, and another UU leader, Annette Marquis, to establish the Living Legacy Project.

Since 2010, the Living Legacy Project has led journeys through the South to meet the people, hear the stories, and visit the sites that changed the country in the civil rights movement. A Living Legacy pilgrimage includes visits to sites in Alabama, Mississippi, and Tennessee, as well as gatherings with movement veterans to learn firsthand about their courage and determination.

A typical journey starts with thirty to forty-five people gathering in Birmingham or Memphis. After an orientation and rest, they embark on a four- to eight-day guided experience, making five or six stops per day to museums, community centers, churches, and historic sites like the 16th Street and First Baptist Churches in Birmingham, the Museum of Peace and Justice, and the Lynching Memorial (which was founded by the Equal Justice Initiative) in Montgomery. Other highlights include the well-designed exhibits at the Mississippi Civil Rights Museum in Jackson and the Emmett Till Interpretive Center in the small town called Glendora, where the murder of Emmett Till took place.

The carefully designed pace of the trip enables participants to see and feel history more accurately than is portrayed in textbooks. Each day of a tour includes lively interactions with residents, organizers, and community leaders who were (and in many cases still are) vibrant agents of action for justice and freedom. Hope's excitement and obvious transformation was intriguing.

A few weeks after our conversation, Rev. Gibson called to formally ask if I would agree to participate in a Living Legacy Project trip that was planned for that October. It would be an eight-day trip and I would be responsible, with pay, for finding ways to connect the participants to the music that had inspired the throngs of people who had filled the churches and marched in the streets at the hallowed spots we would visit on the journey. I certainly knew the songs and was familiar with their use, and I had already been to many of those historic places throughout the years. The conversation went well, and I said yes.

I will admit that I made my first journey with the idea that it would be a one-off gig and that would be that. I was quite busy with my school programs and concert work, and frankly, the pay offered wasn't that great for the amount of time that would be spent. But I figured that it would give me a chance to refresh my memory of the songs and also let me see a few places of interest that my previous travels hadn't covered, such as the Dexter Avenue Baptist Church in Montgomery where Dr. Martin Luther King Jr. had begun his ministry and become an iconic leader of the modern civil rights movement, and the remnants of the store in Mississippi where fourteen-year old Emmett Till encountered Carolyn Bryant in the event that led to his horrific death. It was an event that shook the nation for its brutality and for the mockery of justice in the trial that followed.

Before leaving, I told my agent that I would check in with her three or four times a day during the trip so that we would not be out of touch in case some big, important gigs came through. With that in mind, I flew to Birmingham, Alabama, where we began a trip that would change my life.

Two days into the journey, I began to realize that this was a different experience than I had expected. I had never encountered the iconic civil rights movement sites in the way that the Living Legacy Project presented them. This was an immersion into the heart of the movement that was centered in the narratives of veterans of the struggle, people whose lives were the very embodiment of this history. In their presence, we could feel the emotional vibrancy of that time. It was viscerally affecting, much more so than being on a tour guided by some-one who had simply studied the events of the time.

We heard stories that you don't read in books or learn in school, such as the stories of people who were on the scene the night that Jimmy Lee Jackson was shot in Marion, Alabama. We heard from people who were attacked as children and adults by police in Kelly Ingram Park in Birmingham, or run down, beaten, and tear-gassed on the Edmund Pettus Bridge along with US Representative John Lewis, Rev. Hosea Williams, and six hundred others on Bloody Sunday in 1965. Hearing them tell their stories was a palpable, unforgettable experience that shook me to my core. It inspired me to recall and lead songs from a place in me that felt new and raw. I heard the voices of the elders in my past as my passion came alive, and my heart knew that I had found a new mission.

Informed by waves of these reminiscences, the songs I offered not only brought the history alive for the thirty-five participants on the bus but also served to radically deepen my perspective on the movement. With my heart and eyes opened to a new reality of that period in our national history, I called my agent on Wednesday to say, "I won't be calling you for the rest of the week. Something powerful is happening here, and I'll talk to you when it's over." Before I knew it, I was attending nightly staff meetings to close and review the long days.

I can say with assurance that none of us departed from our final stop in Memphis the same people as when we began. Along the way, we sang together and let the music create a new sense of hope and community, as it did with those amazing civil rights pioneers half a century ago.

After the trip, I was invited to attend meetings to help with the planning of future journeys, and months later I accepted the new position of director of music education with the Living Legacy Project. This enabled the organization to provide participants with a better opportunity to experience the deep resonance of songs and narratives, enhanced by daily conversations and reflections with staff and fellow pilgrims. Within two years, I answered a call to become a member of the Board of Directors, and now I am a co-president of the board with my dear friend Jan Sneegas.

Many people remain unaware of—or are dismissive of—the brilliant leadership that made the civil rights movement possible. True, without the efforts of the millions who marched, protested, went to jail, lost their jobs, and endured inhumane treatment and worse, the gains in rights would not have been possible. But it was the strategic, thoughtful engagement and inspiring actions of people like Rev. Dr. Joseph Lowery, Amelia Boynton, Rev. C.T. Vivian, Ella Baker, Fanny Lou Hamer, Rev. Fred Shuttlesworth, Jo Ann Robinson, and Congressman John Lewis that focused that energy and modeled a way forward for those participants and for American society. Their names are not necessarily ones that the nation knows or celebrates. But their lives were gifts to our country, critical to bringing about civil rights advances.

On one of the earlier journeys with LLP, I had the chance to meet one of my heroes, the Rev. Fred Shuttlesworth, not long before he passed away. His fearless preaching of truth and perseverance in the face of violence and evil has been an inspiration to me. Looking into his eyes that day filled me with a new energy for connecting others to the ongoing struggle for justice.

Since that first trip in 2010, I have been on these extraordinary journeys twice per year on average, at least precoronavirus. I've shepherded hundreds of individuals—from college age to age ninety-four—into a new understanding of civil and human rights. I've seen busload after busload of people who had showed up for what they thought would be a typical tour of historic places slowly find themselves engaged on a deep journey of reflection and transformation. We come to know and appreciate a more personal, emotional, and human side of this national narrative. We reflect on both the repression and the bravery displayed during that time and ponder ways to make a difference in our present world. We are invited to open ourselves to the courage of the people involved in that pivotal movement, often in the face of violence and death, and see what it can offer us as inspiration as we face today's charged racial and political climate. Seeing the sites, singing the songs, and hearing the stories by those who were there strengthens our hope and resolve to become changemakers in our own communities and beyond. We look back to look forward. (Sankofa!)

Each pilgrimage journey has a flow and a spirit all its own. From the number and personalities of the people on the bus, to the regional backgrounds of each group, to the weather, to the stories in the news at the time of the trip, the pace and temperature of each group can be wildly different. The group dynamic is also affected by the ratio of introverts and extroverts and the knowledge base of the participants, so each group can require distinctive timing and approaches.

On one of the early trips, I learned to set up a bit of an office/cocoon in the very back of the bus (ironic, I know!)

where I can listen and observe the group as we move from place to place. When leading, I always go to the front and stand facing the group. I always want to be able to make eye contact as I lead. There are times when I sit with participants to talk, share, and hear their stories. But I discovered that I need to reserve the right to retreat to my cocoon and be aware of how my own emotions are being affected, and to provide a place for my fellow LLP staff leaders to confer with me. I am part of the group, and yet I also know I need to stay slightly out of constant connection so that I can be aware of shifts in the group's energy and any potential problems as they arise. Even with years of experience in leading, every trip has challenges and gifts for me to discover. It's my job to be ready when they present themselves.

In my role as director of music education with LLP, I get to share the deeply grounded history of the music of the civil rights movement, which arose from music that has always been a part of the cultural heritage and tradition of African Americans. I tell our participants that song has long been a means to convey a message, a cultural echo from the villages in Africa. Song has always meant life and connection in the Black community. When people gathered, they sang. It was song that linked them to those who had come before and to those around them in the struggle. The songs gave them a sense of strength and hope that helped them to endure the crushing terror of slavery and Jim Crow and made it possible to endure.

As Dr. Bernice Johnson Reagon pointed out in a 1991 PBS interview with Bill Moyers, "Sound is a way to extend the territory you can affect. Communal singing is a way of announcing you are here and possessing the territory. When police or the sheriff would enter mass meetings and start taking pictures and names, and we knew our jobs were on the line, and maybe more, inevitably somebody would begin a song. Soon everyone was singing, and we had taken back the air in that space."

Singing during the civil rights movement made it easier to get and keep folks involved. Songs calmed people's fears, got them energized, and, when jailed, kept their spirits high and also irritated the authorities. The themes, many biblical in nature, were also relevant to the struggle.

Songs of the movement came from several sources and were not all traditional.

Frequently sung were spirituals such as "Wade in the Water," "Oh Freedom," "This Little Light of Mine," "Ain't Gonna Let Nobody Turn Me Round," and "Woke Up This Morning," as well as adaptations like "Keep Your Eyes on the Prize," "We Shall Overcome," and "The Banana Boat Song." Some of the prominent people who sang them were Fanny Lou Hamer, the Staples Singers, the Freedom Singers, Guy and Candy Carawan, the Carlton Reese Memorial Unity Choir, Harry Belafonte, Pete Seeger, and people at the Highlander Folk School.

The idea of using spirituals—songs composed by people in slavery, also known as sorrow songs—was both simple and ingenious. The religious nature of the songs served the same purpose in the 1950s and '60s as it had in the 1850s and '60s. They expressed the longing for freedom, bolstered faith and resolve, and allowed people to sing in a way that kept the oppressing authorities off balance. They did not include coded messages like the songs in the 1830s to 1860s, but they expressed the faith people felt that God was on their side.

The songs of the civil rights movement had power and purpose. I find myself echoing the words of our friend Pete Seeger (who I continue to miss) who said, "I keep reminding people that an editorial in rhyme is not a song. A good song makes you laugh, it makes you cry, it makes you think! A good song reminds us what we're fighting for."

In March 2015, after I'd been working with LLP for five years, my colleagues and I planned and facilitated a conference in Birmingham called Marching in the Arc of Justice. This conference brought together about six hundred people from around the country to mark the 50th anniversary of Bloody Sunday, to connect people of all ages to the truth of race relations in the past and present, and to plant the seeds of future civil and human rights activity. The conference was an extension of the Living Legacy Project's mission "to re-imagine social possibility by actively experiencing the depth of lessons of the civil rights movement." In stirring sessions with movement veterans, historians, activists, artists, and some family members of those who were martyred, participants reexamined the events that changed America some fifty-eight years ago, with a focus on recommitment and shaping a vision for the future.

Among our featured speakers were civil rights pioneer Rev. C.T. Vivian, Rev. William C. Barber (the leader of Repairers of the Breach, the Moral Mondays Movement, and the former President of the NAACP in North Carolina), and Opal Tometi, one of the founders of Black Lives Matter. I was honored to be charged with setting the tone for the conference by providing music in collaboration with Kim and our friends Greg Greenway, Joe Jencks, and Pat Wictor.

During the conference, Kim, in her new role as college

professor and faith-based academic, reached out to the young leaders of the Black Lives Matter movement in attendance to encourage them to use more music in their protests and to think about the ways that justice movements can flow on a river of song. While the use of song as a tool to build community was used very effectively in the twentieth century, it is less visible in present-day rallies and gatherings.

On the Sunday of the conference, our six hundred conference attendees were bused to a special morning worship service at the City of St. Jude district in Montgomery, Alabama. The City of St. Jude is an amazing complex of educational, social, and medical services and was the site of safety and rest that welcomed Rev. Dr. Martin Luther King Jr. and 2,000 participants of the Selma-to-Montgomery march. The service, which ended with a cascading version of the anthem "We Shall Overcome," prepared us all for the journey back to Selma as we joined 70,000 people from around the world to walk together across the Edmund Pettus Bridge, singing and remembering that hallowed day in 1965. The emotions and sense of purpose I felt as we walked over the bridge were magnified as we came to its apex. I was at once in reverie and overcome with gratitude that no blue wave of troopers was waiting to attack and beat us, as happened to those brave souls fifty years prior. I rejoiced in seeing the diversity that was present in that huge crowd—truly a rainbow coalition of age, race, color, religion, and ethnic background—all singing, crying, smiling, and marching together in solidarity and purpose.

It has become one of my great joys to lead music on these powerful Living Legacy Project journeys that connect people not only to the past but to the critical civil rights issues that still plague our nation. Singing with people on the bus is always one of the highlights that sets the tone for the narratives that we encounter. These songs have stood the test of time and still inspire activism and action to drive us forward.

With so much powerful and heart-rending information being taken in by the participants each day on the journey, it is important to remember that joy and laughter are also a critical part of this process. The heaviness of the topic must be balanced with carefully timed humor and joy. The workers of the civil rights movement were not always serious and somber. Part of self-care was (and remains) the ability to sing and laugh off the weight of the struggle from time to time.

Another avenue of release from the serious topics is food. The fact is that traveling through the South is a veritable smorgasbord of food-related joy. There's simply nothing like a foray through the land of "Honey, are you sure you don't want some more?" to give your mind a break as you sip down another glass of sweet tea!

It remains one of my deepest blessings to be involved in this work. The LLP journeys have provided me with some of the most poignant and challenging moments of my life. The experiences have birthed some of my most joyful moments as well, as I have been more intimately linked to the history and to the people who have made—and in some cases are still making—our movement for freedom and justice possible. It has been a journey of personal transformation that has me singing with renewed inspiration.

> Ain't gonna let nobody turn me round, turn me round, turn me round!

Ain't gonna let nobody turn me round,
I'm gonna keep on walkin,' keep on talkin'
Marchin' up to freedom land.

One of my strong childhood memories is of my mother calling me in from play to watch the March on Washington on TV in 1963. I had no idea where all the places that Dr. King mentioned in his now famous speech were, and I couldn't have imagined that I would see them all in person as an educator and song leader years later.

Since joining the Living Legacy Project, I began to reorder my own connection to the cause of civil and human rights and to rededicate myself to making a daily personal effort to make the world more just. I committed myself to do what I can to get the world one step closer to the dream that Dr. King articulated so powerfully, so many years ago. It changed my reason for singing. It gave me a new sense of what music and story can accomplish. And that was a gift that I didn't expect when I signed on for that first ride on the bus.

CHAPTER SEVENTEEN

THE BALSAM GUYS

When I hit my teenage years, home suddenly felt a lot less safe. Not so much in a physical sense, though there was a growing level of gang violence in Black neighborhoods fueled by the systemic racism and unjust policies of the nation. (Fortunately, I was never pressured to join a gang, though the hopelessness that led to that increased activity and teen violence was hard to miss. I did have to run for my safety on several occasions.) But once I hit adolescence, home became a less welcoming place for me to express my thoughts, questions, emerging desires, and opinions as I grew into my young adult self.

My new independence as a teenager, going to school five neighborhoods away from mine, led to learning new approaches and perspectives from friends and associates. I realized that I was living between two communities, and it was a lonely experience. I was still very respectful to adults and governed by the rules of my early training in most ways, and my strong sense of community accountability was very much intact. But I was beginning to think for myself, which led to my seeing the duplicity in adult actions.

Our home was run as a tight ship, with very strict social, cultural, and religious guidelines. Sharing my evolving opinions or ideas often resulted in fiercely negative reactions from my mom and Nana. Early on, I tried ignoring their reactions and often plunged full steam ahead, expecting that they would understand that this was me being teenage me. That plan, not surprisingly, set up conflicts both vocal and spiritual that had previously been absent from our household.

As a result of these conflicts, I now joined my sister Marlene as a problem to be controlled, which was ironic given that we were both exceptionally good kids—goody-two-shoes-level good kids. Yet I could see from the grief they gave my sister when she took them on that the best course of action for me was silence and stealth. The message I took from Marlene's battles was, "Think what you want, but say very little, and do what you think you can get away with away from the house." She was unable to resist fighting them. But I was more willing and able to go quiet and present a less available presence. I wasn't susceptible to going wild and starting to smoke, drink, or begin raisin' hell, but I was beginning to flex my adolescent muscles. And I wasn't gonna just give in either.

I began testing the rules a bit. In addition to new thoughts, my growing physical strength changed the power dynamics between my mom and me in one significant way. One fateful night, after I came home late from school—I mean *late*, like missed dinner-late—my mother let me know that she was not pleased and sent me upstairs to await the usual punishment, a whipping. After grabbing her big, thick chastening belt out of that special drawer in her bedroom, she came down the hall and commenced the usually effective strokes of remorse. Three whacks in, she watched me stand there and take each blow with a new sense of tolerance that shocked us both. Football and other sports had toughened me. Discovering that she was no longer able to hurt me with a belt was an awkward moment that ended with her saying, "You know I'm not happy." It was a time of change that we never discussed again. And in place of beatings, years of being grounded or lectured to death began.

I was also beginning, in a very confusing way, to discover my masculinity. There's nothing like being a teenage boy living in a house full of women to make you notice that you are other.

My mom was a very loving and giving person, and deep down I knew she was always in my corner. But both she and Nana could be very skeptical and dismissive of men who didn't share their perspectives or meet their established rules of engagement and decorum. Whenever Mom and Nana decided I was too big for my britches, I was told I was being a "belligerent, willful young man." Asserting my thoughts and opinions was, to them, tantamount to falling out of God's will. I wondered, silently, why God's will never included things I wanted to do. Whenever I tried to go beyond the range of their comfort zone, I was sure to hear them exclaim, "OK, Sam Harris! You're actin' just like your father! Hmmmph! Chile know so much. Gonna turn out to no good." To this day I can hear Nana reciting that litany.

Ouch! Just like my father? Buffeted and bruised by their two-fronted attacks, I learned to shut my mouth, go undercover, and hide my feelings.

Just like my father?

I had no way of knowing what that even meant. My dad was not present or accountable to me for all but a few moments of my life. He had married my mother in 1944, but their life together was interrupted by the Korean War. Apparently he returned from the war a changed man, and their relationship soured. They divorced when I was about two. My mother then raised my sister and me, holding down several jobs, working as a seamstress in clothing factories making clothes for boys.

I saw him only three times after his departure. Our final encounter happened at my sister's second marriage ceremony. (I hadn't even bothered to invite him to my own wedding.) He and I had a short encounter on the sidewalk outside of the church right after the ceremony. After greeting each other awkwardly, he attempted to apologize for his years of absence and neglect. I listened to him start his spiel, and then I just cut him off.

"Look, if you really want to have a relationship with me, I'm not hard to find," I barked. "Otherwise let's just call it a life."

I felt the anger of years of abandonment and lost conversations rise up inside me as I blurted out my truth. I had learned through years of fending for myself on the football field or basketball court how to say what needed to be said quickly and directly, like a point guard correcting a teammate in a critical fourth quarter moment of tension. He said nothing in reply, and that was the last time I saw him.

At that moment, I considered the matter closed. I know better now. For much of my early life I had managed to keep the pain of my father's absence at bay. But the hurt was much deeper than I knew and took years to process. That ever-present but hidden ache, and all the solitary moments of telling myself that it didn't matter that he wasn't around, led to suffering that went unresolved for many years.

Counseling sessions later in life got me on the road to unearthing and healing the resentment and pain. I realized that the things I would have liked to have gotten from my father when I was battling all that female energy in the house—to have had some help in shaping conversations, learning or talking about sex (which never happened!), or being coached and encouraged in sports or other traditionally male pastimes—were probably not things he was good at. If he had been, he likely never would have left. But it's clear that his absence affected my ability to develop strong, vibrant male friendships that I could trust.

My mom did try periodically to get me into situations where men were present so I could soak in a little of what was missing in our house, but most of them were with men from our church who, understandably, had limited time for me. They had kids of their own and other family and work responsibilities that demanded their time and energy. They were nice enough to include me in activities or take me to a ball game now and again. They all respected my mom and Nana, and they wanted to make sure that whatever they did or said didn't create any cross-messaging with what Sister Harris was trying to accomplish. Any time I complained about not having a voice or criticized something my mother did or said, they would say things like, "Now, you got to mind your mom. She's got your best interest at heart. She's not gonna lead you astray." Or "Listen to the womenfolk. They know what's what!"

I appreciated the time and attention from these men, but those situations didn't allow me to address things I most wanted to know or heal that ache in my heart. They provided some fun moments and added perspective to my worldview, but they also led me to develop my "I'm a solo free agent" attitude as a coping skill, which was my default position for years.

I got used to being a welcomed but clear outsider to the inner circle of relationships.

When I was in my fifties, in a conversation spurred by some work I was doing in therapy, my sister told me that my dad had claimed before he left our family that I was not his child and had accused my mom of stepping out on him. My mom was not the kind of person who steps out. In fact, I learned from reliable family sources that it was he who had stepped out on her, leaving her for the woman that they had selected to be my godmother. She was never a presence in my life, and I spent years wondering why my sister had a godmother and I didn't. (Yeah . . . nice touch, Dad!)

Marlene's revelation explained a cryptic conversation that my mom and I had shared one night in the early 1990s. She had called me out of the blue (at that time, we talked about once a month or less) to deliver the news that my father had died suddenly. On hearing her rather matter-of-fact statement of his demise, I sat silently on the phone for a moment, absorbing the shock of him being semi-relevant again. I wondered what in my life his death changed.

After a moment Mom asked, "Are you OK?"

"Yeah, I'm fine," I lied. "Are you?"

"Well, I know one thing," she said. "I can say that I've slept well all these years! I kept my vows."

This was a rather shocking statement for me to hear, given that she had never discussed or made comments about her marriage. This was worthy of a sibling conference.

I called and shared that comment with Marlene, and after much discussion, we figured this was her defining moment of satisfaction in her relationship with him. He had thought her unworthy (or told the world she was), but in fact it was the other way around. And now with his death, my deeply spiritual mother was at peace with herself and could move on.

While there were many positive things about being raised as a Black man in a house and a church community led by Black women—being nurtured, guided, corrected, and loved by prominent, strong female leaders—it also served to make my connections to men somewhat distant, untrusting, and conflicted. My lack of connection to and discomfort with male role models was deep and needed to be resolved. I avoided that reckoning for as long as possible.

I realized that I loved but feared women. I'd missed learning about the healthy ways that men and women in relationships can engage with each other. I also doubted myself on many levels.

As a result of a number of friendship and relational betrayals, I had learned to trust very few people, male or female, with my real thoughts and emotions. I was friendly, well liked, and affable, but deeply secretive, self-conscious, and wary when it came down to really being known. Correcting that would take some outside intervention.

With guidance from some good counselors, I began to consciously work on being honest with myself and being a better partner in marriage and in my close friendships. I developed boundaries and learned to keep them. For an open hearted, free-wheeling extrovert like me, who was interested in making friends with the whole world, that was a hard task to take on. Slowly, with guidance and time, I began to understand that having and keeping emotional boundaries worked to make my life more manageable and provided needed clarity about different levels of interaction. For years I had been like a kid in the proverbial candy store of potential friendships and energizing human connections, looking into the case and choosing one of those, and one of those, and two of those with no attention to what might already be in my bag.

It became clear to me that, as a public person, every connection I made or encounter I had could not have the same intensity or duration. Further, the person who needed to monitor my own openness and accessibility was me. By protecting the sanctity of my close relationships and making them more of a priority, those relationships became more trusting and took on more depth. I also began to notice a sizable reduction in the outflow of energy I expended day to day. All of this was a revelation that opened my ability to be a true friend and partner, while still being thoughtful, kind, and present to those I met along the way at gigs.

As my level of fame grew, this took on more significance. Role models like Pete Seeger and others of my more famous friends offered thoughtful and efficient ways to be present but not needy. One friend said, "Remember always that you're just a person, regardless of how they might see you from the stage. Look them in the eyes and *see them* as a person. Then, being careful not to buy into whatever your promo has created, honor the moment and move on."

I also began to foster collaborations centered in honesty and respect with fellow musicians, male colleagues, and other male connections. I learned to say what I meant and to stand by it. That had always been true on the sports side of my life, but now I saw reason to expand it into my everyday life.

On the advice of a friend, I happened into an experience

with a remarkable group of men (and two women) at the Omega Institute's yearly Beyond Basketball workshop held on Labor Day weekend that was led by Phil Jackson (of Chicago Bulls Championship fame) and his friend, writer Charley Rosen. The thirteen years I spent as part of that close circle was groundbreaking not only in helping me work through some of my male trust and collaboration issues, but it also really helped my game. At the same time, I volunteered as a Big Brother to serve as a role model for a young man whose relationship with his father was troubled. It was both a sobering and rewarding relationship that continues, more distantly, to this day.

I found progress and joy in taking these critical steps in my life, and it helped me become more comfortable relating to other men and finding confidence in myself. Then, almost out of the blue, came the experience that has helped me to put all of that learning into a new life practice: being part of a men's group called the Balsam Guys.

The Balsam Guys men's group began with a work friendship I developed with Michael McCarthy, who was the youth director for the Roman Catholic Diocese of Rockville Center on Long Island, New York, when we met. Michael had seen me in a performance with Kim at a youth event in Philadelphia and was taken with our energy and message. He later hired us to co-lead retreats for his groups. Our discussions on life, faith, religion, music, world events, and whatever else came to mind were always deeply engaging, but also brief because they usually happened at meals and breaks sandwiched between workshops. Time after time we would engage on some topic, only to be frustrated and somewhat amused by our inability to ever finish a conversation. Finally, after sharing yet another limited conversation during lunch at a conference in Birmingham, Alabama, we laughingly said, "This has to stop!" We resolved to reserve a weekend in which we would meet and talk until we were talked out.

Unable to keep this to ourselves, each of us mentioned the idea to a few trusted male friends, three on each side, who in turn were intrigued by this idea of a group of guys getting together to talk, and they all wanted to join in. The eight of us committed to gathering for a weekend in 1999 on the eve of Y2K at a small family retreat center.

Michael, his brother Robert, his best friend Phil, and his brother-in-law David came from Long Island and New Jersey. I invited Ed and Tim, two friends I knew through music connections, and Mike, a friend who was a social worker in the act of becoming a filmmaker, all from the Albany area. We arrived at Balsam Shade Conference Center in Greenville, New York, on a Friday afternoon, each of us filled with anticipation and a little doubt.

From moment one, the synergy was evident. Conversations and connections deepened with every hour and the bonds grew quickly. In a remarkable coincidence, two of the guys had been to Balsam Shade in their youth with their families and said it was like coming home.

In the group are two teachers (now retired), a filmmaker, two New York State workers (both now retired), an advertising executive (also retired), a construction executive (still on the job), and me (musicians seldom retire—we just try not to die on stage!). I am the only person of color and also the only non-father in the group, though our diversity is otherwise quite remarkable. We use our life experiences, our listening skills, and our vast array of personal gifts as we plunge deeply into the issues and idiosyncrasies of trying to live with grace, passion, and honesty as men in this society. We are deep-thinking men who are also playful, joyful, serious, comical, self-deprecating, and curious. We are also privileged in that none of us has experienced homelessness or many of the other societal deprivations that plague so many people in our nation.

We meet once a year, gathering on a Friday by dinnertime. We eat a meal together and then begin a weekend of personal sharing of the status of our lives, with only a few important rules:

1. Everyone gets a turn to talk about their life uninterrupted for up to an hour during each gathering.
2. Whatever we share in those minutes must be personal and an honest reflection of the issues and concerns presently driving our lives.
3. The group can ask, probe, reflect on, challenge, or offer support on what is shared throughout the weekend, either in the group or privately, as time and protocol allow.
4. Whatever is shared during the weekend is to remain confidential unless the sharing member gives permission for public airing or discourse.

Over the years, through openness and patience, trust has grown. We have never chosen a theme for our weekends, but it always seems that whatever topics arise evolve organically into useful explorations of matters that are critical to all of us. On more than one occasion, the group process has caught me trying to avoid an issue or brought me into an awareness that I would not have come to on my own, much to my benefit. Such was the case of our gathering in 2002. Without prompting, the first three men shared reflections about unresolved family issues and challenging family relationships. I remember saying to myself, "Oh, damn! I don't want to spend the entire weekend talking about family relationships." At the time, my own family relations—particularly the state of my arguments with my mother—were a sore point, and I had been looking forward to this weekend as a chance to get away from thinking about them. But when the next two guys who shared continued with this theme, I knew the writing was on the wall. I felt trapped, but trusting their lead, I leaned in.

Since I was one of the last slated to share on Sunday morning, I had time all day Saturday to gather my thoughts. After the powerful sharing of our evening session, I said goodnight to the guys and went to my room where, despite the long, active day, I found it hard to fall asleep. I picked up my guitar, pulled out some paper, and tried to make some notes that I thought might lead to a song. Instead, wide awake and annoyed, I found myself starting to write a letter to my father. What the hell?

I tried to resist the process but soon, unable to control the flow, I was writing furiously, with words and thoughts filling the page faster than I could think. Eventually, tears of anger were replaced by deep sobs of sorrow, and the salt and convulsions began to hurt my eyes and ribs. I could feel the residual shards of my painful non-relationship with my father find their way to the surface and out into the room.

The feelings I was wrestling with were captured beautifully in the poem titled "How Do We Forgive Our Fathers?" by Dick Lourie:

maybe in a dream: he's in your power
you twist his arm but you're not sure it was
he that stole your money   you feel calmer
and you decide to let him go free

or he's the one (as in a dream of mine)
I must pull from the water but I never
knew it or wouldn't have done it until
I saw the street theater play so close up
I was moved to actions I'd never before taken

maybe for leaving us too often or
forever when we were little   maybe
for scaring us with unexpected rage
or making us nervous because there seemed
never to be any rage there at all

for marrying or not marrying our mothers
for divorcing or not divorcing our mothers
and shall we forgive them for their excesses
of warmth or coldness   shall we forgive them

for pushing or leaning for shutting doors
for speaking only through layers of cloth
or never speaking or never being silent

in our age or in theirs or in their deaths
saying it to them or not saying it—
if we forgive our fathers what is left?

Just after 3:00 a.m., spent, still weeping, I felt my strong emotions ebbing and sensed that whatever I had been keeping bottled up inside of me for years had been released. Mercifully, I fell asleep and was late for breakfast.

In our session that morning, I read my tear-stained letter to the guys. As they so often do, they enveloped me with love. Their support and thoughtful questions allowed me to find a deeper level of release and resolution. They joined me as I said goodbye to the haunting memory of my father, but not before they also made a few critical challenges that helped me launch a reconciliation and healing journey with my mother.

I had no way of knowing that within the next year my mom would enter a hospital for what was pegged as an easy operation, contract an infection, and subsequently lapse into a coma and die. But in the last months of her life, our relationship blossomed as we put to rest many of the conflicts that had kept our relationship in turmoil since my childhood years. At her funeral in our home church in Philadelphia, I looked around the church in a hard, grief-filled moment and was shocked to see that every single one of my Balsam Guys was there, in the balcony, seated as a group. They had come, without notice, to honor my mom and to help me close out that chapter of my life. There they sat, present for me as friends and as brothers as they have been throughout each year—in person, by email, phone call, or text, or with cards sent at just the right time.

For twenty-three years we have gathered in person at about five different locations—except in 2020 and 2021, when the pandemic prevented us from meeting in person. During the pandemic, we met online in Zoom sessions that mirrored our interactions when we gather in person—time set for singular sharing and then collective reflections and support. Fortunately, we resumed our in-person gatherings in 2022 and were able to once again enjoy all of the things that are so meaningful to us—our meals together, our walks, our picture sessions, our poem readings, and the late-night political, book, or cultural discussions over snacks and laughter. The hugs, the sitting in silence, and the tears that flow without any sense of guilt or shame. The sound of our voices together in one room and the easy flow of chatter around the table at meals.

Over all these years, we have shared in each other's moments of joy and confusion, acknowledged depression, celebrated moments of career success, pondered personal and medical challenges, and wept in times of sorrow. The guys saw me through the twelve years of the liver illness that culminated with my liver transplant, and they have provided me with a safe space in numerous career and health difficulties, in times of relational crisis, and in my launch of a solo career. We have spurred each other to action in dealing with race, prejudice, and educational and spiritual disaffection and have held each other accountable in our social, marital, and personal commitments to making ourselves better citizens and servants to the world.

We chose the name Balsam Guys because of that small family retreat center where we got our start. But the name signifies more than just a place. It reminds us that we have grown deep roots and that together we stand tall and strong, like a grove of balsam trees. As our lives change, having that sturdy support to lean on and that root network to draw from is priceless. Our commitment to each other is a sacred bond, an unwritten covenant that is more than I could have ever asked for when I sought a new way of relating to men. The group has enabled me to acknowledge, process, and move on from the pain, anger, and emotional scars in my life and restored my reason to trust men. The Balsam Guys are, one by one and all together, a gift beyond measure.

CHAPTER EIGHTEEN

TOWARD SOLID GROUND

As I began writing this book in March 2020, the coronavirus pandemic had just made its presence known in United States. Politically, the country was stuck in a quagmire of deep division, fear, and anger exacerbated by the misinformation and posturing of the Trump administration. As the country shut down due to the pandemic and life as we knew it came to a halt, I suddenly found myself at home, with all of my performances and school shows canceled. At first I felt disoriented and disheartened. But soon a silver lining emerged. With hours of solitude every day, I revisited the routine of my 2008 liver transplant recovery and found a peaceful mindset and the perfect opportunity to reflect and write. As Linda and I began to gather material for this book, I was also encouraged by friends and fans to do some online concerts. Before long, every day was a creative frenzy of online concerts and community sings, new book chapters, and original songs flowing out like water.

The onset of the pandemic was quickly followed by a long series of high-profile events that shone a glaring spotlight on the racial issues rife in America, including:

- A rash of racist attacks against Asian people fueled by the Covid-19 outbreak

- Ahmaud Arbery being shot dead while jogging in Georgia
- Breonna Taylor being shot dead while asleep in her bed in a botched police raid
- The Covid-19 pandemic disproportionately impacting people of color
- A White woman calling the police on a Black man, Christian Cooper, birdwatching in Central Park
- George Floyd being killed after a Minneapolis police officer kneeled on his neck for nearly nine minutes
- Confederate statues being toppled in the South
- An Atlanta police officer shooting and killing Rayshard Brooks in a Wendy's parking lot
- Jacob Blake being shot in the back at point-blank range seven times by a Wisconsin police officer
- Jonathan Price being shot dead by police after trying to intervene in a domestic dispute
- A mass grave being discovered in Tulsa during search for massacre victims of the 1921 Tulsa race massacre

In reaction to all of the above, protests were taking place across the country calling for justice and police accountability and reform. During this time, I had to turn off my phone for several hours a day due to the volume of emails, texts, and calls that flooded in asking me for a conversation or to be part of a Zoom panel to discuss why America is so divided. When I checked in with Black friends and colleagues, every Black performer, lecturer, and public educator I know shared that they were receiving a similar volume of opportunities to weigh in and give perspective.

On the one hand, most of us were thrilled that these incidents, which have been part of our lives and awareness for decades (sigh), were suddenly on America's radar. We felt some hope that these events would provide clarity, would constitute a great reckoning with racism that could lead to true change and evolution. So we took the calls.

On the other hand, the events of that time weighed heavily on me and my fellow people of color. The emotional toll of seeing the violence and feeling the pain was often overwhelming.

I had more than a few days in which staying in bed and eating chocolate seemed the best option. My Black colleagues also felt a need to seek cover at times.

As a nation, we've been engaged in a passion play of deception in regard to race relations for over three hundred years. While eight years of tenuously glimmering hope with the election of our first Black president, Barack Obama, made it seem to the untrained eye that we were on the road to redemption and renewal, that dream was dashed in the vicious backlash unleashed by the 2016 election of Donald Trump. Over the four years of the Trump administration, countless unholy, unethical, and emotionally abusive examples of greed, narcissism, collusion, hate, evil, and dysfunction became bitter daily accompaniments to our lives. The flames of racial discord and hatred were stoked, causing an uptick in public rage and mistrust.

However, in the midst of the turmoil of 2020, I experienced a personal renewal of hope, born out of my belief in the power of song and my belief that a world in which love is the measure of action, belief, and policy will be one in which justice, abundance, and equality are paramount. In my pandemic solitude, I returned to the spirituals. I sang them to myself. I shared them with my audiences online. I let the words fill my head and heart once more.

> Wade in the Water. Wade in the Water, Children.
> Wade in the Water. God's gonna trouble the water!

The elders clapped and shouted and called again:

> Ain't gonna let nobody turn me 'round
> turn me round, turn me round.
> I'm gonna keep on walkin'
> Keep on talkin'. Marching up to freedom land.

When the political discord and the steady stream of police killings of Black people became overwhelming, I found that through singing—alone and with others—I began to lose my own fear, uncertainty, and confusion. I began to believe again that my voice, added to the voices of others, would help to turn the tide of hate, giving us the energy to organize, march, campaign, rise up, and vote against the current of injustice and indifference that had the nation in its grip.

With the wild events in the news as fuel, I began writing songs that explored how the historical and social narrative of our past fits into our current times. The first song I wrote in 2020, "It's Who We Are!" rose from a powerful and therapeutic exercise of introspection and creativity. I was writing to fashion a response to the cacophony of questions that came from White people following the deaths of George Floyd, Breonna Taylor, and other revelations of injustice. (How did we get here? Isn't America the "light on the hill"? Weren't race relations getting better with Obama? Where did all this violence come from? Is this new?)

The answer, to anyone who had been paying attention, was clearly no. This ain't close to being new. It's who we are, and who we have been for all of our nation's history.

> You can blame the politicians, you can blame your neigh-
> bors too
> You can blame the founding fathers for what their mothers
> didn't do.
>
> Well, the answer is quite simple, it's not hard to recognize.
> It's greed, it's self-indulgence, it's the fear of compromise
>
> In the light of introspection where the truth is known to be
> It's our choices that betray us, it's the lie that says we're free.
>
> So, we turn to face each other and we say "Why, Why, Why?
> How did we get this way? It's who we are!"

And then another new song, "On Solid Ground," rose out of me. This song, written in the frame of the spirituals, was imbued with energy and wisdom of the elders and put our present-day challenges into context and perspective.

> It's been a long hard journey on a winding road
> So many have gone before us and they carried a heavy load
> But they went there singin' as they made their way
> Now we follow their footsteps as we work today.

I know that you're weary . . . we all feel the pain
Sometimes the actions of the world will try your soul again
But I believe that a better day is comin' our way
That's why we're raising our voices as we work today.

All around there is hatred . . . all around us there's fear
Violence touches our lives and the message is clear
We mourn our martyrs . . . in our hearts they stay
As we sing "We Shall Overcome" and go on our way!

We will not rest till the storm is over
We will not lay this burden down
We will keep each other strong
We will love and carry on
Till we stand all together on solid ground.

With that song, I found my mojo in full working order again. Eventually I realized that I had compiled enough songs to make an album. I cautiously began to make trips to the studio—with Covid safety measures in place—and a year later, the album *On Solid Ground* was born. When it was released in May 2021, it received wonderfully gratifying reviews and found its place as one of the most-played albums in folk radio circles that year.

While it is critical to acknowledge that hate and divisiveness remain at the core of our embattled national narrative, it is also true that a groundswell of resistance is growing in response to the racial disparities and injustices that were laid bare in 2020. A new movement is underway, comprising people of all ages. I am thrilled to be a voice in that struggle.

Despite the heart-wrenching news stories that stream from media sources every day, I see glimmers of hope. I believe we are journeying toward solid ground, as witnessed by the big, bold, and needed backlash against centuries of police violence and brutality toward African Americans following the horrific deaths of George Floyd, Breonna Taylor, Ahmaud Arbury, and so many others. I see progress in the conviction of the three men who murdered Arbury and in the sentences of the policemen who showed such stunning disregard for the life of George Floyd.

I am encouraged by the reckoning with centuries of institutionalized racism, inequity, and patriarchy that colleges, universities, corporations, and nonprofit organizations are undertaking. I see a continued commitment by more and more organizations and corporations to rebuke White supremacy. The toppling of statues of confederate generals (including my great-great-great grandfather W.C. Wickham) and the removal of other symbols of the Confederacy in cities and towns across the country indicates that there is a rising consciousness of the injustices that exist in America. I am cautiously hopeful that we might, over time, find a way to reject the politics of division.

The rising empowerment of Millennials, Gen Xers, and the emerging Gen Z, with their willingness to demand change and accountability, has amplified my sense of hope. We are seeing more women, more people of color, and more young people of conscience running for public office. Survivors of school shootings like David Hogg from Parkland, Florida, Zoe Touray from Oxford, Michigan, Eliyah Cohen from Los Angeles, Taina Patterson of Miami, RuQuan Brown of Washington,

D.C., and many more are using their voices, actions, and organizations to affect change.

I'm happy to say that, in my world of folk and acoustic music, where audiences and presented artists have been historically heavily White (and also less than diverse in other important aspects of equity such as gender, sexual orientation, and ability), awareness and commitment to these issues seem to be growing, although it often requires direct conversation and advocacy to bring about change.

An example of this took place in 2019 when I was blessed to be brought in by my friend Joy Bennett as an instructor for Trad Mad, a wonderful weeklong adult music and dance camp held at Pinewoods Camp in Plymouth, Massachusetts, for folks who love to sing and learn traditional song, storytelling, and dance. It was not my first time there, but this time was a little different. I arrived to teach three courses and to interact as a camp participant for the week. As things came to be, I was the only person of color, staff or student, in the place.

As I've mentioned, since my teen years it has been a very normal thing for me to have to negotiate situations where I am one of a few, or the only, person of color in a group. I have put myself out there, sometimes because I'm asked to perform to aid a cause, sometimes because I want to do something or go somewhere that isn't attractive to most people of color. And the truth is, sometimes I do get weary. Sometimes the burden of representing the race feels like too much. There are times when being the only one, or everybody's first conversation with a Black person, drains me to the core. Times when I've had one too many episodes of having to answer the question, "How do Black people feel when . . ." And sometimes an incident in the world or a personal encounter will drain my resiliency tank to low, especially if I have not been connected enough to my own cultural framework. Yes, sometimes I do get weary. And it was like that at the end of summer 2019 when I arrived at Trad Mad to discover that I was the sole person of color.

Before the first all-group convening I ran into my dear friend Scott Ainslie, a fine musician and White social justice ally. He asked me, "How does it feel to be representing the race again?" We had a conversation in which I told him that it felt very exhausting at that moment. Scott, with whom I have done many programs and have shared deep conversations about race and music, graciously listened, and then pledged to support me in whatever ways I needed. He offered not only to speak to my needs that week, but also to bring it up with leadership. As it turned out, Joy Bennett and Heather Wood were more than supportive, and the week went by with many a fine moment.

Later in the fall, Joy and I engaged in several more conversations about the critical aspects of attracting and actively welcoming more diversity in the community. She pledged to make this more of a focus in her programming, not only at Trad Mad but also at the Old Songs Festival in Altamont, New York, which she now directs. Within a year, Joy's actions on our conversation were evident in the look and feel of both events. An increased number of performers of color and additions to the workshops demonstrated her commitment to the concerns we discussed. I also learned from other sources that she had extended our conversation to other performers and festival sponsors and has become an active ally in the effort to be more inclusive.

In 2020, Alastair Moock, a White musician friend from

Boston, emailed to ask if we could have some conversations about race in the aftermath of the George Floyd murder. He shared that he was already part of a collection of diverse artists who were taking on the subject with a group called Family Music Forward. Those artists were discussing the fact that the 2020 Grammy nominees in children's music were, once again, all White. They talked about making changes that could bring attention to and overcome this long-standing racial injustice. Alastair and two of his fellow White nominees (the Okee Dokee Brothers and a group named Dog on Fleas) decided to reject their award nominations and request that the Recording Academy undertake a review to make the process more inclusive and equitable. Their protest resulted in groundbreaking social change within a year.

Joy's and Alastair's responsiveness are only two of many examples that fuel my hope. For the last eight years, Aengus Finnan, the former executive director of Folk Alliance International (FAI), led that organization into a deep examination of, and a practical engagement in, building more equitable policies that give access to performers and music that are not so narrowly homogenous. I've served on FAI committees with a number of my colleagues and have helped lead many listening sessions both at FAI and with my union, Local 1000, aimed at changing the paradigm that has been in place for so long.

A key ingredient in bringing about change is increasing the awareness of mainstream members who hold power and who are unaware that the structure caters to White privilege. It is necessary to approach actions with thoughtful critique and discernment, since the cultural and systemic structures of organizations generally mirror the larger society. Real change requires shifts in power that are often hard to effect, given that the lack of balance in numbers favors the majority in decision making. I've been pleased to see some movement within FAI, but as with the general struggle for change, I know that this is a long road.

Getting older, and my epiphany during my liver illness and transplant journey, has loosed my tongue, making me less willing to be a silent partner or sufferer in the ghetto of the token few people of color. After years of making a statement simply by my presence, I welcome having more of a chance to speak out and share the wisdom that comes from years of performing and comparing notes with BIPOC colleagues. The openness and commitment of my colleagues to make change happen fills me with hope. I have also learned to gracefully say, when needed, "Yeah, I'm tired. I'm going to take some time off. How 'bout you work this frame for a bit?" I don't need much room to say what I think. Nor do I need to take much time off to rest from the struggle.

I am filled with hope as I watch college students find new purpose and become voices of change through their involvement with the Living Legacy Project. On one Living Legacy Project pilgrimage in January 2019, fifteen students of color from Nazareth College began to realize the merits of sharing their anger and pain with their White colleagues after two days of singing, getting in touch with their emotions, and seeing truth on the bus. For their part, the White students on the trip had great difficulty in hearing that their unconscious privileged actions (both on the journey and back on campus) were the source of pain and turmoil for their travel companions of color. When the groups gathered into separate spaces for discussion, the White students were perplexed, hurt, and anxious. Bringing the students together, my LLP colleagues, the Nazareth College staff, and I were able to encourage a series of one-on-one dialogues and group reflection sessions between the groups. Slowly, as channels of communication opened, evidence of learning and trust began to surface that, with continued nurturing back on campus, was still in evidence months later. Nazareth College continues to send students on LLP pilgrimages and bring me to campus to talk and sing with students. With my recent visits to the College of Wooster in Ohio, St. Joseph's University in Philadelphia, and other colleges, this restorative work is spreading to other campuses around the country.

Further evidence of healing was revealed during the pandemic as I witnessed efforts by my White Wickham cousins, who met online for weeks to reckon with their family history following the murder of George Floyd and the toppling of our ancestor's statue. Their discussions and subsequent decision to establish a family-funded scholarship (and to explore other ways of giving back from their privilege) has been a fascinating process to observe. Among the beneficiaries of their action are student scholars from the Virginia Foundation for Community College Education. In mentoring sessions that I've had with the scholars, the students described with joy that they feel empowered to take ownership of their own narratives and futures after hearing the stories of my Hewlett/Wickham connection.

My hope has been inspired in part by my friendship with Pete and Toshi Seeger. Pete told me once to remember to "sing more when things are at their worst." Toshi showed me that courage comes from being prepared, fearless, and decisive when faced with bravado that is meant to instill fear. Toshi Seeger didn't take no stuff.

My sense of hope was also inspired by my mother, Helen Harris, who was a hopeful person and showed great resilience in the face of adversity. Born in 1920, my mom and her family came through some very difficult times with the challenges of racism, injustice, and the turmoil of the Depression as a backstory. She lived an existence of faith, discipline, and moderation, with many periods of struggle. Her life was not easy, and I realize now that observing her attitude and manner of handling her reality has helped me shape my own perspectives and values.

So, with renewed hope, I dedicate myself to the cause, working to bring about the day when we are, all together, standing on solid ground.

CHAPTER NINETEEN

SANKOFA

Sankofa is a concept derived from the Akan people of Ghana that means "one should remember the past to make positive progress in the future." The word Sankofa literally means "to retrieve" in the Akan Twi language.[4] That idea is that one can and should reach back to pull forward useful things from the past that are at risk of being lost.

I am constantly reaching back to reclaim the decency and respect for democracy that was lost during the Trump administration. I also reach back to the glorious music that filled my church as a child as I create and share music with others. I reach back to all of the great elders—Martin Luther King Jr., Rosa Parks, Eleanor Roosevelt, and Harry Belafonte, to name a few—and to the musicians, poets, and civil rights pioneers to retrieve their spirit of common humanity, courage, and compassion. I reach back, striving to follow their examples of perseverance and determination, to help all of us move forward toward the solid ground of justice, peace, and equality.

It can be hard to remember that *we* are the good news. If we realize that we still can open our hearts to honest

---

4 "Sankofa Meaning: What Is the Ghanian Concept About?" MasterClass, https://www.masterclass.com/articles/sankofa-meaning-explained

connections that bind us to each other, then the world will change for the better. Whether it's talking to a stranger on a plane (when we can safely do that again!), talking to the young people we love to help them make sense of what's happening in the world, volunteering an hour or two at a school, a soup kitchen, or a community center, or helping people register to vote, we can help build the kind of society we want to live in. If not us, then who?

In my work, I see my roles of messenger, listener, musical connector, cultural ambassador, and collaborator as open ended. One of the enduring messages I took away from my training at the National Coalition Building Institute was that we were not being trained to go out to change people's minds. If we do our job effectively, we create windows of opportunity where participants can feel safe to consider some new information about themselves and others that might lead to a shift in their perspective. When that new information connects to who they are and how they feel, they will change their minds and their behavior. Keeping this in mind, I try to offer a new perspective and leave space for connections to happen, while also being true to who I am and to my own well-being. I hold lightly to the fact that I might not see the end result of any one interaction. I try to share what I know, think, or feel in ways that invite others to see themselves as part of the ongoing human story.

That approach, along with many years of practice, has served me well through decades of struggle, challenge, joyful exploration, illness, and triumph. And they have fueled movements of social and historic change in which I find myself, with renewed vigor and without fear, working on the front lines. We are living in a challenging time. We have much work to do. But with all of us working together and music at our center, I believe we will rise up for justice. I believe Rev. Dr. Martin Luther King Jr. had it right when he said, "Darkness cannot drive out darkness; only light can do that. Hate cannot drive out hate; only love can do that."

As my musical career and life have evolved, I have become part of a multi-hued fabric that is strengthened by the efforts of friends, colleagues, and mentors of all races, colors, and backgrounds who are taking up the banner of justice in their own way. I join with others in a commitment to try to make the world more inclusive, honest, and peaceful. They, along with the elders, stand with me now, in mind and heart. It is in their names that I say I dare not lose hope. I dare not lose faith. I dare not allow others to silence my voice.

Looking back on my life, I see the sweeps of multiple journeys of transformation. Like the colors of a rainbow, the arcs of these journeys nestle one against the other.

- My journey from a poor, Black choir kid to a national touring musician performing in concert halls, schools, colleges, and coffeehouses across the nation and the world
- My journey from declaring "I have no people" to attending the Million Man March and proudly embracing my Black identity
- My journey of meeting and getting to know my white-skinned Wickham cousins.

- My journey serving as a cultural ambassador—reaching across age, ethnicity, social location, background, and national borders—to bring music, healing, and hope
- My journey of moving from the diverse city of Philadelphia to the not-at-all racially diverse rural community of Middleburgh, New York
- My journey from death's door to renewed health through the gift of my liver transplant
- My journey from a musician who just came to share a few songs and stories from a time long ago to becoming one of the co-chairs of the Living Legacy Project and using my voice to fight for justice, equality, peace, and civil rights for all

I am grateful to you, my readers and fans, for having accompanied me on these journeys. They represent what has been a remarkable evolution for me. I had not planned to make the struggle for civil rights and justice a major life focus when I first dreamed of life on the musical road. I had no idea growing up that this type of life was ever possible. But the cumulative effect of all my life experiences, and the times we are living in, has imbued in me a sense of commitment that cannot be shaken. The constant thread through all of it has been music. For me, music is the source of life and hope. It is my gift, and it brings me alive day after day. It is the gift that I am blessed to share with you.

> We will not rest till the storm is over
> We will not lay this burden down
> We will keep each other strong . . . we will love and carry on
> 'Til we stand all together on solid ground.